Their finest hour

D0986104

the story of the Battle of Britain 1940

Edward Bishop

Their finest hour

BB

Editor-in-Chief: Barrie Pitt
Art Director: Peter Dunbar

Military Consultant: Sir Basil Liddell Hart
Picture Editor: Robert Hunt

Design Assistants: Gibson/Marsh
Cover: Denis Piper
Research Assistant: Yvonne Marsh
Cartographer: Gatrell Ltd
Special Drawings: John Batchelor

Edward Bishop is the author of The Battle of Britain published by Allen & Unwin in 1960 whose permission for the author to base this book on previous research is gratefully acknowledged

First printing: May 1968
Printed in the United States of America

Ballantine Books Inc.
101 Fifth Avenue, New York, NY 10003

Contents

High Summer, 1940

Introduction by Barrie Pitt

At the conclusion of his most famous wartime speech, Mr Churchill used these words 'The Battle of France is over . . . the Battle of Britain is about to begin. Upon this battle depends the survival of Christian civilisation. Upon it depends our own British life and the long continuity of our institutions and our Empire.'

These words contained a higher element of historical truth than is usual in public orations. In the late summer of 1940, Britain alone could still offer defiance to German power and rejection to Nazi philosophy – for she alone, of the powers who had at last taken up arms against Hitler, remained unconquered. The only other powers who could offer him physical resistance, Russia and the United States, were prevented from doing so by blindness where power lay in their respective political systems; neither Stalin nor the American public saw, as yet, why the existence of Nazi Germany posed threats to their own way of life.

At this time, therefore, Britain played a vital part in world history – possibly more vital than ever before, almost certainly more vital than ever again.

In those long summer days of 1940, as Edward Bishop so graphically describes, the Battle of Britain appeared to us here as an affair of high gallantry, of laughing youth going gaily to battle, and white vapour trails high in a clear blue sky; in one London suburb a bailed-out RAF fighter pilot was enthusiastically kissed by the entire staff of the laundry in which he landed, while on the coast the local police had to fight to save shot-down Luftwaffe pilots from lynching at the hands of fishwives.

These elements were present. But behind them was the industrial effort which gave Britain the Spitfire (triggered originally by the imaginative enterprise of Lady Houston – surely one of the most historically significant contributions ever made by a single individual) and the inventive genius which gave us radar. Wars have always been decided more by the quality of weapons and equipment than popular feeling has allowed, and the more industrialised the world has become, the greater the factor played by technical skill in comparison with the ancient virtues of bravery and strength. This aspect too, Edward Bishop's book brilliantly illustrates: the Battle of Britain was eventually won by the ability to climb high and fast, to shoot straight, and even more important, to be in the right place at the right time.

France falls

In Berlin it seemed almost unbelievable. France, the old enemy, had fallen to the army and the Luftwaffe. The low countries of Belgium and Holland had been overrun, Denmark occupied and Norway defeated after a short and bitter struggle, while to the east less than a year before, a victorious German army had buffered Berlin from Moscow, conquering Poland in a matter of days.

It had all been so easy, a German walkover, and now in the year 1940 as summer came to Europe the German people could reasonably expect that Britain would seek peace on Berlin's terms.

Certainly, as he concluded armistice arrangements with France's elderly Marshal Petain in late June 1940, Adolf Hitler, the idolised Fuhrer, had presented Germans with every reason to expect miracles.

Employing a bizarre touch which was both in character with his perverted sense of destiny and a delight to a vengeful fatherland, Adolf Hitler had brought the defeated French to the forest of Compiegne, to the very railway coach in which France had obliged Germany to grovel in 1918.

Here, Adolf Hitler, more powerful in Continental Europe than Napoleon at the zenith of his success, descended skittishly from the railway coach followed by his field marshals; this amateur, the little corporal who had defeated France where the Kaiser and all his glittering staff had failed. It was a glorious vengeance after years of struggle and imprisonment, for Hitler had returned from the first world war, determined to avenge the treaty of Versailles and the terms imposed on Germany by the victors of 1914-1918.

But, between Adolf Hitler and his ambitions for Germany, there was the Royal Air Force of Great Britain, or at least what remained of it after the fall of France and the British Army's evacuation from Dunkirk.

The British, much to Germany's astonishment, were fighting on. In late May and early June they had pulled back from the Continent to their little island, leaving all of their armour and equipment behind. But now in late June they were defiantly bracing for invasion across twenty-

**Dance of victory: Hitler by the
railway carriage at Compiegne**

9

Pageant of defeat: French and British prisoners after the fall of Dunkirk

11

two miles of choppy sea and, as it seemed to Germans, hopelessly, suicidally prolonging the war.

Surely the British must soon face up to their desperate situation and accept the futility of further resistance? Their island was beleaguered from the Bay of Biscay to the Norwegian fiords by an invincible Luftwaffe.

As Germans saw things, the Royal Air Force – what remained of it – was outflanked and outnumbered; and without air cover the Royal Navy, however powerful and courageous, could not save Britain from blockade or invasion. On land, the cities and industries of the United Kingdom were wide open to the Luftwaffe. Surely to fight on was foolhardy and purposeless? The German people contented themselves that even at this late stage the British must see reason. Give it a few more days and the war would be over.

But one man in Germany was not so sure. Adolf Hitler was uneasy about Britain and that ridiculously defiant little fly, the Royal Air Force. Early in his struggle and long before he came to power in 1933, Adolf Hitler had formed an opinion of the British people and their qualities, and he had registered it in his personal political testament, MEIN KAMPF. 'Britain can be counted upon to show the brutality and tenacity in its government, as well as in the spirit of its broad masses, which enables it to carry through to victory any struggle that it enters upon, no matter how long such a struggle may last, or however great the sacrifice that may be necessary, or whatever the means that have to be employed; and all this even though the actual military equipment at hand may be utterly inadequate when compared with that of other nations'.

It was scarcely surprising, therefore, that holding this opinion Hitler should privately doubt the successful outcome of his public peace overtures in June 1940, and on July 2 he ordered the preparation of provisional plans for the invasion of England. In so doing he retained his misgivings about the wisdom of attacking Britain but temporarily permitted the recent performance record of Hermann Goering's Luftwaffe to overlay it. Goering, Reich Marshal and Luftwaffe Commander-in-Chief, was confidently predicting that his Luftwaffe could win victory over Britain's fighter defences in a matter of days. Hitler went along with the dream. Certainly, he found Goering's optimistic forecast more palatable than Grand Admiral Raeder's naval warnings against invasion. Moreover, as he was already contemplating the conquest of Russia in the following spring the German Fuhrer was attracted to Goering's aerial knockout blow. Possibly it would avert the need for opposed landings, possibly it would bring Britain to his peace table where she might be enlisted as a junior partner in a crusade against communist Russia.

But, if opposed landings had to be made, then so be it. The Luftwaffe after gaining total air superiority would neutralise the threat of interference by the Royal Navy and speed the German army on its march on London. In the spring the Luftwaffe had thrown the army across the Meuse and forward to Paris and now, in this high summer of success what was the Channel other than a somewhat longer and more turbulent crossing?

Early in July the Luftwaffe, refreshed and re-equipped after its continental victory, was ready to resume full scale operations. Relaxing at Karinhall, his country home outside Berlin, Hermann Goering waited impatiently to launch the air force's three air fleets against Britain.

As he manoeuvered toy trains around the track of his magnificent model railway the Reich Marshal planned the 'attack of the Eagles' that would subjugate Britain.

Germany's view was that Britain and France had presumed to declare war on her as she marched into Poland. The Luftwaffe had quickly disposed of Poland, and now France had fallen. Next, Britain would learn that Germany had forged an air arm capable of producing victory within weeks, even days of the launching of an offensive.

Indeed, Hermann Goering was so confident of the Luftwaffe's ability to bring off a single-handed conquest of Britain that he showed no interest in army or navy invasion planning. Two

German air fleets, Air Fleets 2 and 3, were standing by in France, Belgium and Holland, while a third and smaller air fleet, Air Fleet 5, was stationed in Norway and Denmark. Between them the air fleets comprised more than three thousand bombers and fighters, a large enough force the Luftwaffe Commander-in-Chief was confident, to eliminate Britain's invasion area air defences in four days and to end the war in as many weeks.

As the fighters and bombers waited in their forward airfields, Hermann Goering could reflect with pride on his creation of the chief instrument of German conquest. Peacock vain about his record as a fighter pilot with twenty-two credited victories in World War I, Goering had prospered the fortunes of the new air arm as Germany's Air Minister after Hitler's seizure of power in 1933. However, the real ground work had been completed earlier by the army professionals, among them Field Marshals Kesselring and Sperrle and General Stumpff, the very same Luftwaffe leaders who were now facing England in command, respectively, of Air Fleets 2, 3 and 5.

Exploiting a loophole in the Versailles Treaty the professionals had forged their weapon before Hitler and his Nazis came to power. This had not been difficult. While breaking up the German Flying Corps of the first world war the allies had failed to regulate the future of Germany's civil aviation. Permitted a defence organisation under the Treaty, Germany had entrusted the army high command to General von Seeckt, an officer who fostered close liaison with civil aviation and laid the foundations of the Luftwaffe in 1921 – aided by those young men, Kesselring, Sperrle and Stumpff. There had been others, too, who had risen to power with the air fleet commanders and now found themselves riding comfortably on the Luftwaffe's lightning success. Among others high in the Luftwaffe command were Erhard Milch, late of the civil air line, Lufthansa, and in 1940 deputy Commander-in-Chief of the Luftwaffe; Ernst Udet, equipment chief; and Hans Jeschonnek, Chief of the Luftwaffe General Staff. Nor in the years between the wars had German aircraft manufacturers been slow to see their new opportunities. The result was that, in the summer of 1940, the Dornier, Junkers, Heinkel and Messerschmitt aircraft standing ready to reduce Great Britain, owed their parentage to the soldiers and industrialists who had been preparing this act of revenge for twenty-one years.

As early as 1928, and neatly tucked away in Sweden, the Junkers company built a dive-bomber, the fore-runner of the Stuka, the Ju 87. By 1935 a prototype Ju 87 was flying in Germany – and failing from tail flutter – powered by a Kestrel engine from Rolls Royce, the famous British automobile company. In 1933, Ernst Udet was experimenting with a pair of Curtiss Hawk dive-bombers he had bought from the United States. Nor did fighter development lag behind. As early as 1935, an Me 109 was going through its paces, powered by a Kestrel engine from England.

But the air fleet leaders and their aircraft were not the only products of Germany's secret rearmament; the commanders at lower levels and many of the men who were about to fly against England had begun their careers at camps and flying fields concealed from the Allies.

From 1924, selected officers were despatched to Lipetz, a flying training school in Russia. Many of the German officers who were to hold important commands in the Battle of Britain of 1940 had passed through Lipetz in civilian clothes. Others, wearing Italian uniform, had trained in Italy by courtesy of Benito Mussolini, the Italian dictator.

In 1926, at the instigation of von Seeckt, Lufthansa had been established as a state monopoly airline under the chairmanship of Erhard Milch, an air hero of the 1914-18 war. In 1940 Milch was a General and keenly disappointed that the Luftwaffe had been reined back since the evacuation of Dunkirk.

In Lufthansa, von Seeckt's defence organisation had exploited a first class training ground for Germany's future air force. Lufthansa aircrew doubled their civil duties with military instruction.

It was not until 1935 that the Luftwaffe finally came into the open

Reich Marshal Hermann Goering C-in-C Luftwaffe

F.M. Kesselring C-in-C Air Fleet 2

F.M. Sperrle C-in-C Air Fleet 3

Gen Stumpff C-in-C Air Fleet 5

Gen Milch Deputy C-in-C Luftwaffe

15

Top Messerschmitt ME-Bf109 E-4
A formidable opponent for the RAF's Spitfires and Hurricanes – but over-extended by the long-range flights over Britain, forced to cover ME-110 fighters as well as the bombers, and finally grossly misused as a fighter-bomber. *Speed:* 357 mph. *Max range:* 412 miles. *Armament:* two 20-mm cannons and two 7.92-mm machine-guns.

Middle Junkers JU-87 A-1 Stuka
In close support of the German army during the Blitzkrieg campaigns in Poland and France, the Stuka had made history as 'flying artillery'. It could pinpoint targets with deadly accuracy, but only in the absence of fighter opposition – and it therefore suffered drastic losses in the Battle of Britain. *Crew:* two. *Speed:* 199 mph. Max range: 620 miles. *Bomb load:* 1,100 lbs (pilot only). *Armament:* two 7.92-mm machine-guns.

Bottom Heinkel HE-111 H-3
The Battle of Britain was the first campaign which rammed home Germany's failure to develop a long-range heavy bomber to do the work done by planes such as the HE-111 medium bomber. Like the JU-88, it was also used as an anti-shipping strike aircraft. *Crew:* five. *Speed:* 254 mph. *Max range:* 1,100 miles. *Bomb load:* 4,000 lbs. *Armament:* five 7.92-mm machine-guns, one 20-mm cannon.

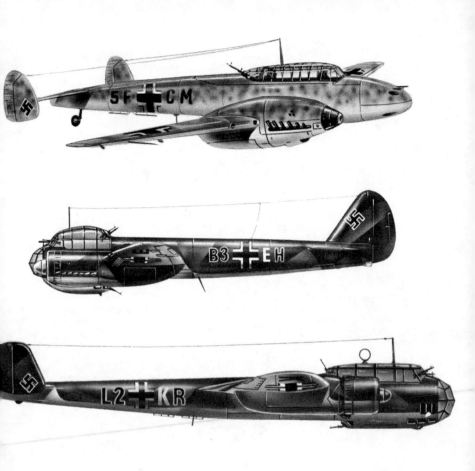

Top Messerschmitt ME-Bf110 C-1
Goering hoped that 'destroyer' formations of ME-110s would carve through all fighter opposition, cleaving a path for the bombers – but the 110 was far too heavy and sluggish to 'mix it' with the Spitfire and Hurricane, and suffered accordingly. *Crew:* two. *Speed:* 349 mph. *Max range:* 565 miles. *Armament:* five 7.92-mm machine-guns and two 20-mm cannons.

Middle Junkers JU-88 A-2
Maid-of-all-work for the Luftwaffe, serving as dive-bomber, level bomber, night-fighter, and reconnaissance. It also served with distinction in the torpedo-bombing role against Allied convoys. It suffered – like all German bombers – from a chronic weakness in defensive armament. *Crew:* four. *Speed:* 286 mph. *Max range:* 1,553 miles. *Bomb load:* 3,963 lbs. *Armament:* four 7.92-mm machine-guns.

Bottom Dornier DO-17 Z-2
The DO-17 was a lighter, slimmer plane than the HE-111. Like the Heinkel, it had been blooded in the Spanish Civil War: like all Luftwaffe's bombers, the Battle of Britain forced it to carry out operations which proved the inadequacy of its design. *Crew:* five. *Speed:* 265 mph. *Max range:* 745 miles. *Bomb load:* 2,200 lbs. *Armament:* six 7.92-mm machine-guns.

Tools of victory: Ju 88's on the production line

Ju 87 'Stuka' flying for the Condor Legion in Spain during the Civil War. This was great combat practice for the Luftwaffe.

under Goering, Milch and other comrades of the first world war; as the most powerful air force in Europe, ready to test its men and machines in support of Franco's insurrection against the republican government of Spain. It was a successful trial.

In Spain Luftwaffe units under Hugo Sperrle and Wolfram von Richthofen, cousin of the celebrated fighter ace of the first world war, compensated for Franco's shortage of artillery. Here, von Richthofen's Ju 87 Stuka dive-bombers rehearsed the tactical close support of tanks and infantry which produced the new and terrifying warfare – Blitzkrieg – and placed Air Fleets 2 and 3 within flying minutes of Britain's front line airfields. In Spain, too, combat experience developed Luftwaffe pilots destined for future leadership, among them Adolf Galland and Werner Mölders who were shortly to become legendary figures. As part of Germany's Condor squadrons they practised the close army support operations which subsequently spearheaded Germany's victories of 1939 and 1940 in Poland and France. The Luftwaffe made the most of its training opportunities in Spanish skies, exchanging raw volunteers from Germany with civil war 'veterans' to spread experience throughout the service.

With so much behind him, Hermann Goering was contemptuous of contingency planning for an opposed invasion of England. It was a waste of effort. In his judgement the Luftwaffe's eight hundred Me 109 fighters, three hundred twin-engine Me 110 long-range destroyer fighters, four hundred Ju 87 dive-bombers, fifteen hundred Dornier, Heinkel and Junkers bombers, rendered invasion planning redundant.

At Karinhall, impatiently increasing the speed of a toy passenger express thundering round the model circuit, the Luftwaffe's Commander-in-Chief wished heartily that it was the special train in which he was to be conveyed to the channel coast to witness the end of Britain.

Hitler, however, could not bring himself to take the irrevocable step while peace without conquest might still be possible. On July 16, two weeks after ordering a provisional plan for invasion, he issued Directive 16, a more thorough invasion brief; 'As England, despite her hopeless military situation, still shows no sign of willingness to come to terms, I have decided to prepare, and if necessary to carry out a landing operation against her. The aim of this operation is to eliminate the English motherland as a base from which war against Germany can be continued and, if necessary, to occupy the country completely'. No date was set. Invasion was still only a matter of contingency planning.

While the army, the navy and the air force obeyed the Führer's orders and made their preparations, the German people could not believe that Britain would be foolish enough to invite invasion. The Berlin newspapers were almost certain the war was over. 'The whole of England is trembling on the brink of a decision,' the evening newspaper *Nachtausgabe* declared. 'There is only a slight possibility of England offering any military resistance . . . The British people are in downright fear of forthcoming military and political events'.

Victory flags, victory music, victory gaiety – the Führer had relaxed his dancing restrictions on Wednesdays and Saturdays – all combined to convince the people that it was over; some Generals too. Rommel wrote to his wife from France,' By my estimate the war will be won in a fortnight. Lovely weather – if anything, too much sun'.

Hitler hoped the optimists were right, but were the British really likely to give in without a fight? Summer campaigning weather was passing with every day. There was but one course of action; to put peace overtures to a final and dramatic test, and if they failed, to unleash the Luftwaffe and to give Goering his opportunity. On July 19, 1940, Adolf Hitler addressed the world:

'In this hour, I feel it to be my duty before my own conscience to appeal once more to reason and commonsense, to Great Britain as much as elsewhere. I consider myself in a position to make this appeal since I am not the vanquished seeking favours, but the victor speaking in the name of reason. I can see no reason why this war must go on. I am grieved to think of the sacrifices which it will claim. I should like to avert them also for my own people . . . Possibly Mr Churchill will again brush aside this statement of mine by saying it is merely born of fear . . . In that case I have relieved my conscience with regard to the things to come . . . Mr Churchill ought for once to believe me when I say that a great empire will be destroyed – an empire which it was never my intention to destroy or even to harm. I do, however, realize that this struggle, if it continues, can end only with the complete annihilation of one or other of the two adversaries. Mr Churchill may believe that this will be Germany. I know it will be Britain.'

Britain digs in

In London, Winston Churchill was contemptuous of Adolf Hitler's appeal to reason, and foolishly so as it seemed outside Britain. After years of exile in the political wilderness, years in which he had consistently warned successive British governments of the menace of a re-arming Germany, Churchill had replaced Neville Chamberlain as Prime Minister on May 10, 1940 – the very day, as it happened, of Hitler's invasion of France and the low countries.

Thus in a few short weeks Winston Churchill had seen the worst of his fears realised. He had seen the Luftwaffe punch the German army through to the channel coast and the Royal Air Force whittled down in the process. But, excepting its application to an adversary, surrender was never a word to be found in his vocabulary – although in his wisdom he respected the pessimistic opinion of outside observers and the reasons for it. He broadcast 'I can easily understand how sympathetic onlookers across the Atlantic, or anxious friends in the yet unravished countries of Europe, who cannot measure our resources or

resolve, may have feared for our survival when they saw so many states and kingdoms torn to pieces in a few weeks or even days by the monstrous force of the Nazi war machine.'

Speaking at Pearl Harbor, Colonel Knox, the US Navy Secretary and a friend of Britain, was to endorse Churchill when at the height of the battle he said, 'The chances of British victory are now better than fifty-fifty.'

After the fall of France, Churchill told the nation, 'What General Weygand called the Battle of France is over. I expect the Battle of Britain is about to begin. Upon this battle depends the survival of Christian civilisation. Upon it depends our own British way of life, and the long continuity of our institutions and our empire. The whole fury and might of the enemy must very soon be turned on us. Hitler knows that he will have to break us in this island or lose the war. If we can stand up to him all Europe may be free and the life of the world move forward into broad sunlit uplands. But if we fail, then the whole world, including the United States,

RAF display. Hendon 1937

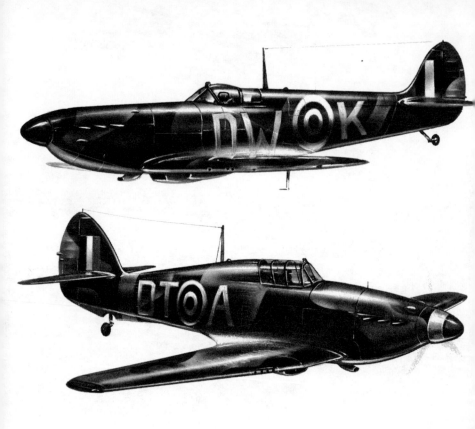

Top **Supermarine Spitfire 1A**
In August 1940 there were only 19 Spitfire squadrons in RAF Fighter Command, compared
to 29 Hurricane squadrons – yet German pilots rapidly learned respect for the tight-turning
Spitfire, which had the same high fire-power as the Hurricane. *Speed:* 362 mph.
Max range: 395 miles. *Armament:* eight .303-inch Browning machine-guns.

Bottom **Hawker Hurricane Mk 1**
Although the Hurricane was the numerical mainstay of RAF Fighter Command in the Battle,
it was already being replaced by the Spitfire as Britain's first-rank fighter. Well able to deal
with the ME-110, it was usually outclassed in combat by the ME-109. *Speed:* 336 mph.
Max range: 443 miles. *Armament:* eight 303-inch Browning machine-guns.

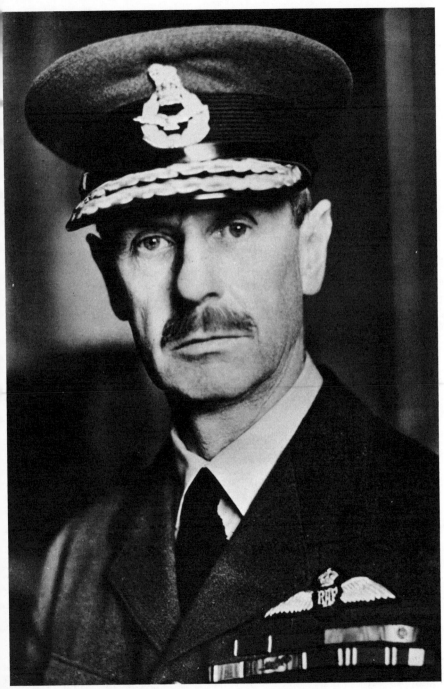

Air Chief Marshal Sir Hugh CT Dowding, GCVO, KCB, CMG.,
C-in-C RAF Fighter Command

including all that we have known and cared for, will sink into the abyss of a new Dark Age made more sinister, and perhaps more protracted, by the lights of perverted science. Let us therefore brace ourselves to our duties, and so bear ourselves that, if the British Empire and its Commonwealth last for a thousand years, men will still say, "This was their finest hour."'

Taking office on May 10, confronted immediately by the invasion of France and shortly afterwards by the evacuation of a retreating British army bereft of most of its military equipment, Churchill had been granted no time to repair the mistakes of his predecessors; to prepare for the battle which he feared must now reach across the channel, and which he had already anticipated in name as the Battle of Britain.

Behind Winston Churchill's stirring and timely call to the nation there lay a long and sorry tale of British governmental unwillingness to meet the alarming reappearance of Germany as a menace to world peace; and in consequence a barely respectable defence against air attack – even before the fall of France.

Indeed, but for the personal ingenuity, private philanthropy, public spiritedness and sheer merchant adventure of a number of individuals and aircraft companies, the Royal Air Force would not have been equipped with *any* machines as fairly competetive with their Luftwaffe counterparts as the Spitfire and Hurricane fighters. In 1936, when the Luftwaffe was preparing its new Do 17, He 111, Ju 87 and Me 109 modern monoplane aircraft, tested a year later in the Spanish civil war, London was guarded by biplanes.

In a 1936 exercise for the defence of London's key fighter airfields, Biggin Hill, Hornchurch and North Weald, the Fighter Command of the Royal Air Force mustered three squadrons of Bristol Bulldogs, four squadrons of Hawker Furies and one squadron of Gloster Gauntlets. When Neville Chamberlain returned from Munich in the autumn of 1938, out of thirty operational fighter squadrons one was equipped with Spitfires and five were re-equipped with Hurricanes.

If in the uneasy years preceding the outbreak of the second world war the Luftwaffe had its dedicated professionals whose experience, as that of its Commander-in-Chief Hermann Goering, reached back to combat in 1914-1918, the RAF was not without its leaders from the Royal Flying Corps of the past.

The difference was that such officers as Air Marshal Sir Hugh Dowding, research and development chief in the critical early to middle 1930s, had to contend with political leaders who were not preparing for war. Lacking government enthusiasm and financial generosity Dowding and his colleagues were at a disadvantage to their Luftwaffe counterparts.

Nevertheless, although prototype Spitfire and Hurricane fighters were not ordered until 1934 and 1935 respectively, the British Air Force professionals had not been idle. But the evolution of the Spitfire and the Hurricane derived as much from a string of romantic incidents and plucky gestures as from defence planning. It was an odd story.

In 1927 and 1929 while the seeds of the Luftwaffe were still being sown under cover, the Royal Air Force had won the Schneider Trophy, the coveted prize for a biennial international race for seaplanes. A third victory in 1931 would give Britain permanent possession of the trophy. But on economic grounds the British government barred the Royal Air Force from competition. It seemed likely, therefore, that the RAF would have to accept the ignominy of watching the United States or possibly Italy fly off with the trophy. Then, the wealthy, eccentric Lady Houston offered £50,000 towards expenses. The government shamefacedly relented and the RAF, flying an aircraft which was the mother of all the Spitfires, won the race and retained the trophy. The air marshals seized their opportunity. Orders were placed for two separate prototype fighters to specifications relating to the Schneider experience.

It was a race against time. The plane that won the 1931 Schneider Trophy had come from the drawing board of RJ Mitchell, chief designer of the Supermarine Company, and Mitchell was a dying man. On holiday in Germany after a serious operation,

Mitchell met German air enthusiasts and returned full of foreboding about the future. He knew that he was working against the clock on two accounts, his failing health and a re-arming Germany. In his anxiety Mitchell worked on two machines – the first to meet the government's restrictive and retrogressive specifi-cations and the second, the true Spitfire, to meet his own and the Supermarine Company's vision of what a modern fighter ought to be. Reginald Mitchell died, aged 42, in 1937 shortly before the first production Spitfire took the air.

From Sydney Camm of Hawker's came the Hurricane. Camm was delighted to escape from biplanes, the value of which he had long disputed with the Air Force who were still in-fluenced by a 1912 committee report which had ruled that monoplanes were unsafe.

Considering that time was against them it is remarkable how Mitchell and Camm narrowed Germany's lead. They were, after all, meeting new problems throughout, problems affec-ting the new era of the monoplane and its refinements; including retractable undercarriages and such new aids to flying as radio and blind flying cockpit instruments. They were entering, too, a new era in aero engine power with the supersession of the Kestrel, so keenly experimented with in Germany, by the magnificent Rolls Royce Merlin. There was also the question of relating armaments to the speed of modern fighters; the arrival with the Spitfire and the Hurricane of the eight-gun fighter.

On the credit side, however, was the comfort that amid all the trials of leap-frogging several years of re-search and development, Mitchell and Camm were supported strenuously by their companies. At Supermarine, a subsidiary of Vickers Aviation, the Vickers associate company's chair-man Sir Robert Mclean shielded Mitchell from government inter-ference, especially as he was secretly building the true fighter, the one the government had not ordered.

There were other aircraft in the coming battle, as this account will show – the Blenheim bomber, for example, impossibly cast in a fighter rôle, and the obsolete Gladiator biplane. But these aircraft were far surpassed by the outstanding co-stars of the Battle of Britain, the Spitfire and the Hurricane.

To the immense relief of the Air Force, the prototypes of the two new fighters revealed their promise on their maiden flights – the Hurricane on November 6, 1935 and the Spitfire on May 5, 1936. By December, 1937, the Hurricane was coming into squad-ron service but the first Spitfires were not available for operational flying until June 1938.

Gradually, the new Hurricanes and Spitfires replaced the obsolete Gaunt-let and Gladiator biplanes which guarded Britain and were no match for the modern fighters and bombers of the Luftwaffe. As the old guard handed over, squadron for squadron, no man was more relieved and delighted than Dowding who, in the summer of 1936 had been moved from research and development to head as Commander-in-Chief and to build a defence organi-sation worthy of the new aircraft, the new Fighter Command of the Royal Air Force. The entire air defence of the nation became Dowding's respon-sibility. In addition to the fighter squadrons of the RAF the Commander-in-Chief, Fighter Command, exercised operational control over Anti-Air-craft Command, Balloon Command and the Observer Corps – later the Royal Observer Corps.

Dowding's frustrations over the re-equipment of the Royal Air Force were numerous and vexing as he worked to provide Britain with an efficient system of defence.

At the start, as the fifty-four year old Air Chief Marshal moved into headquarters at Bentley Priory, an historic mansion at Stanmore on the northern outskirts of London, he had to contend with a defeatist policy. In 1932, Stanley Baldwin stated: 'The bomber will always get through . . . the only defence is offence which means that you have to kill more women and children more quickly if you want to save yourselves'. And, by 1936, the year in which Dowding arrived at Fighter Command, Stanley Baldwin had become Prime Minister.

Regarded as too defensively minded, Dowding was uncomfortably aware

Harbinger of war: London sees its balloon-barrage being tested for the first time. Summer 1939

that at any time he might expect to be retired prematurely; that as British service people say, a bowler hat was permanently suspended over his head. Passed over as Chief of the Air Staff, the most senior appointment in the Royal Air Force, Dowding, a stiff, uncompromising character (nicknamed 'Stuffy' by his contemporaries) was not popular at the Air Ministry where policy decisions were made. There was scarcely a detail in his new defence system over which Dowding was not obliged to struggle, including a request for concrete runways to make grass airfields serviceable in all weathers. The Air Ministry was against all-weather concrete runways on the grounds that they were awkward to camouflage. Not until war was imminent did the authorities relent and allow Dowding his concrete. To that point he had been obliged to experiment with grass seeds to ensure that grass airfields were at least sown with the most suitable grasses.

In another altercation with the Air Ministry, Dowding, fighting for bullet proof windscreens for his Spitfires and Hurricanes, made the inspired argument, 'If Chicago gangsters can ride behind bullet-proof glass I see no reason why my pilots should not do so too.'

Yet, Dowding's critics could not understand why the fighter chief called for so much sophistication in planning even though Stanley Baldwin had warned in 1934, 'Since the day of the air, the old frontiers are gone. When you think of the defences of England you no longer think of the chalk cliffs of Dover, you think of the Rhine. That is where our frontier lies.' Baldwin's statement was intended to justify such meagre rearmament as was taking place. Meanwhile, Hitler was building an air force capable of placing the German army and the Luftwaffe advance air bases twenty-two miles from the white cliffs of Dover.

Nevertheless, despite all difficulties Dowding built a defence system which, while unprepared to cope with an enemy at Calais and by no means foolproof, managed to save his country from invasion and defeat when the test came in 1940.

The success of the system depended on Dowding's determination, and here

The watch on the sky:
Observer Corps post

Operations room staff plot approach of enemy raiders

he was technologically ahead of his time, 'to apply science thoughtfully to operational requirements.'

Control and standardization were the orders of the day. Identical operations rooms were established at Fighter Command headquarters in the Groups and in the Sectors into which Dowding divided his command. As early as 1936 Dowding realised that in the event of war, in the event of daylight attacks on Britain, he was likely to be out-numbered and short of fighters. Therefore he designed a flexible system whereby, in the vulnerable area of southern England, fighters could be passed from sector to sector, from group to group by operations room staffs elaborately linked by telephone and teleprinter lines.

As he strove to prepare Britain against attack, Dowding was kept short of money. In 1936 he received a mere £500 to build an experimental operations room in the ballroom of Bentley Priory. Later, only £4,500 was allowed for an underground bomb-proof headquarters.

But such parsimony seemed almost excusable providing one new development was not refused cash. This was radar, radio direction and ranging, or as it was known in its primitive days, radio direction finding, Britain's secret shield, and as it transpired the very salvation of the country. As No 60 Group, the new radar chain also came under Dowding's command.

Bizarrely, the thin, novice radar chain which Dowding fostered and linked to his defence control system emerged from a far-fetched suggestion that raiding bombers might be disintegrated by a science fiction type of death ray. Sceptically in the mid 1930s the defence scientists investigated and reported, as they knew they must, that no means existed of generating beams of sufficient power to break up bombers; but they held an ace up their sleeves. If the radio beam as a magical killer was nonsense, the radio beam as a long range direction-finder was a practical possibility.

Among the Royal Air Force's scientific advisers was Robert Watson-Watt who had devised a radio means of locating thunderstorms. He had bounced radio waves off storms and from the ionosphere and he now

Beaverbrook:
Minister of Aircraft Production.

succeeded in bouncing them back from distant aircraft. It so happened that Watson-Watt's early experiments were taking place while Dowding was responsible for Air Force research and development. Thus, by the time Dowding moved to the newly created Fighter Command, he had already helped to introduce the chain of tall three hundred feet masts which was being built along the east and south coasts of England.

The Luftwaffe, rightly, was inquisitive about these mysterious masts. Working as it was on its own research into the distant detection of aircraft, and suspecting that the sprouting masts related to similar activity, the Luftwaffe attempted to investigate.

Enterprisingly, General Wolfgang Martini, the Luftwaffe's signals chief, had persuaded Hermann Goering to recommission the retired Graf Zeppelin as a flying laboratory. It was a bright idea because no existing aircraft could have supplied the range, the room and stop-look-and-listen manoeuverability essential to this new departure in aerial reconnaissance. Nevertheless, the spying proved abortive. The airship made several cruises along the English coast but her elaborate equipment failed to function adequately. After a final attempt early in August 1939, the Luftwaffe abandoned this vital reconnaissance.

Preoccupied almost immediately by its leading role in the invasion of Poland, Norway, Denmark, France, Holland and Belgium, the Luftwaffe lost interest in the British radar masts. Rendered over-confident by its

Communications centre

RADAR: BRITAIN'S FAR-SEEING EYE

Dowding's chain of radar stations could locate enemy bomber formations as they built up over France, and so alert the AA and fighter defences. This was radar's main contribution to the Battle. The technique, still in its infancy, tended to under-estimate the number of aircraft on the plot, and was especially weak at low altitudes. The vertical sweep, which located the height of the target, is shown in light grey; the horizontal sweep, which located the target's bearing, in dark grey (centre)

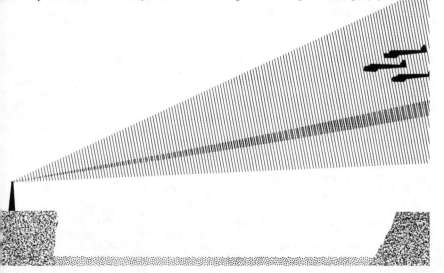

continental victories and expecting a dictated peace with Britain, or at worst another rapid conquest, the Luftwaffe paid little attention to Dowding's radar chain in its evaluation of Britain's chances of survival after the fall of France.

The Luftwaffe's confidence, foolish in retrospect, seemed legitimate enough in the early summer of 1940. The Royal Air Force had suffered grievously in France and was in no condition, Goering supposed, to re-equip and defend Britain against continued air attack. The Luftwaffe was not, as yet, familiar with the bulldog spirit of Churchill or the old warrior's moves to save existing fighter aircraft and build new machines while France was falling.

To speed the production of Spitfires and Hurricanes the Prime Minister enlisted, as he termed it, 'the vital, vibrant energy' of Lord Beaverbrook, the Canadian-born proprietor of the London Daily Express, appointing him Minister of Aircraft Production.

To conserve Spitfires and Hurricanes the Prime Minister forbade reinforcement of the RAF in France. Refusal of fighters in France's final agony was perhaps Winston Churchill's most sorrowful action in that long and eventful career. Without Dowding's dramatic appearance at a War Cabinet meeting, it is doubtful if Churchill would have ordered it.

Appalled by rising RAF fighter losses in France – two hundred and fifty Hurricanes lost between May 8 and May 18 – Dowding sought permission to appear before Churchill and his Ministers. On May 13 he had been ordered to send thirty-two more Hurricanes across the channel, while on May 14 the transfer of ten more squadrons, or one hundred and twenty Hurricanes, was being considered following an urgent request from the French Premier, Paul Reynaud.

In his appraisal of the situation Dowding was not alone. The combined chiefs of staff of the Royal Navy, the Army and the Royal Air Force reported to the Prime Minister under the ominous heading, BRITISH STRATEGY IN A CERTAIN EVENTUALITY.

'While our Air Force is in being, our Navy and Air Force together should be able to prevent Germany carrying out a serious seaborne invasion. Supposing Germany gained complete air superiority, the Navy could hold up an invasion for a time, but not for an indefinite period. In these circumstances our land forces will be insufficient to deal with a serious invasion. The crux of the matter is air superiority. Once Germany had attained this she might attempt to subjugate this country by air alone. We should be able to inflict such casualties on the enemy by the day as to prevent serious damage, but we cannot be sure of protecting our large industrial centres from serious damage by night attack. If the enemy presses home night attacks on our aircraft industry, he is likely to achieve such material and moral damage as to bring all work to a standstill.'

'While our Air Force is in being . . .' Everything rested on the qualifying phrase. Dowding could not stand by and allow his small savings, only thirty-nine Spitfire and Hurricane squadrons, to be squandered on what was obviously a lost cause. With less than 1,300 pilots – some 150 below establishment – he had to preserve his pilots too. On May 15, the Air Chief Marshal walked into the Cabinet room. Placing an explanatory graph on the table Dowding told the Prime Minister, 'If the present rate of wastage continues for another fortnight we shall not have a single Hurricane left in France or in this country.' Spitfires were not mentioned. They were so precious that, until the Dunkirk evacuation of the British army, there was no question of Spitfires leaving home.

On May 19, Winston Churchill directed that no more fighter squadrons were to go to France, except to cover evacuation. Churchill's response to Dowding's plea enabled Fighter Command to see Britain through the Dunkirk evacuation between May 26 and June 4. Even so Dowding had lost more than four hundred and thirty Spitfires and Hurricanes between May 10 and Dunkirk.

Now the questions of the hour were – how long would Hitler hesitate and how soon would Beaverbrook's appointment as Minister of Aircraft Production bring results? Fortunately or Britain, while Hitler was telling von Rundstedt in France 'I will make peace with England and offer her an alliance. Germany will dominate Europe and England the world outside,' Beaverbrook was waving a magic wand over the fighter factories.

His expedients, if unorthodox, were publicised in his own daily newspaper and good for civilian morale. Beaverbrook had not been long in office when he launched an appeal 'To the Women of Britain':

'Give us your aluminium ... We will turn pots and pans into Spitfires and Hurricanes, Blenheims and Wellingtons. I ask therefore that everyone who has pots and pans, coat hangers, shoe trees, bathroom fittings ... made wholly or in part of aluminium ... should hand them over at once to the local headquarters of the Women's Voluntary Services'.

The rest of the press took up the cry, 'From the frying pan into the Spitfire' ran the inevitable headline. In practice, the mountains of saucepans collected by housewives made little practical contribution to the production of fighters but Beaverbrook's appeal was worth its weight in bathroom fittings in terms of civilian morale. Ordinary people, women in their kitchens, bewildered by the turn of events, felt that here at last was something they could do. Fighters, fighters and more fighters ... national survival would depend on Spitfires and Hurricanes. In the month preceding Beaverbrook's May 14 appointment as Minister of Aircraft production, or Aircraft Minister as he characteristically preferred to be known, the factories had built two hundred and fifty six first line fighters. In the critical month of September, 1940, as London came under daily aerial bombardment and RAF losses reached their zenith, Beaverbrook's production and repair organisation delivered four hundred and sixty seven fighters.

To achieve such startling results so rapidly – an average monthly production of nearly five hundred fighters – Beaverbrook maddened the 'bloody air marshals' as he collectively named the air staff at the Air Ministry. He threw overboard their meticulously drawn up and balanced production programmes which looked good on paper but were wholly unrealistic in the desperation of the hour. Two professionals reckoned it a ruthless intrusion by an outsider and Marshal of the Royal Air Force Sir John Slessor later commented, 'The bloody air marshals were supposed not to know what was good for them, and the new minister lost no time in producing a new production programme, based solely on the capacity of the industry to churn out aircraft; it bore little or no relation to strategic requirements, and the main idea (perhaps natural in a man who knew nothing about air matters) appeared to be to produce enormous quantities of fighters, quite regardless of the consequential effect upon other no less vital types. The less spectacular essentials, such as trainers, spare parts and the meticulous phasing of indispensable ancillary equipment do not look so impressive on a graphic chart and tended to go to the wall'.

In all government war departments senior civil servants were shocked by Beaverbrook's display of administrative fireworks. Hardly had they recovered from the blow that this extraordinary fellow believed summer holidays were somewhat out of place in the circumstances of 1940, when they discovered that he expected them to lay down their pens and use the telephone to get things moving. Worse, he brought in some brilliant business men and production engineers, notably Patrick Hennessy, then General Manager of the Ford Motor Company in Britain, and Trevor Westbrook, late of Victoria, whom he found on a golf course and out of work.

In his relations with the United States, where he was already buying aircraft before May was out, Beaverbrook the Canadian who spoke almost the same tongue, acted as quickly and impulsively. When Henry Ford personally intervened in a deal and refused to permit his company to build Rolls-Royce Merlin engines on the grounds that they were weapons of war, Beaverbrook switched the order to Packards. Disregarding experts who warned that Packard was too small a business for the order, Beaverbrook simply said, 'Make it larger' and they did.

Into battle

Balloons over Dover

May moved into July and by July 10, the day from which Britain historically records the Battle of Britain, the Luftwaffe while still on Hitler's leash, was pawing playfully at channel shipping and along the inviting invasion coast of southern England. Britain, it seemed to the German High Command, was still in shock after her Dunkirk experience and incapable of understanding the unpleasant truth of her situation. She might yet come round and talk peace. In the meantime it could be only advantageous to tease and to stretch the fighter defences of the Royal Air Force, or what remained of them.

Amid high excitement among the well-rested Luftwaffe crews along the coastline of northern France, Belgium and Holland, the fighters were armed and the bombers were loaded up. Britain was passing convoys through the Channel, British ports and naval bases in the south of England remained inviolate. Peace or no peace, the all-conquering Luftwaffe might as well demonstrate that this channel was no longer an English

moat; indeed that the channel was no longer English. To the German air force it seemed an easy task. In good weather the cliffs of Dover were clearly visible from Luftwaffe observation posts, and the ships that sailed between bobbed in the channel like toy boats on a public pond. Easy targets. Throw a few stones and they would sink. On July 10 the Luftwaffe selected a convoy.

Slowly, just after lunch the merchant ships in convoy heaved abreast of Dover and immediately Dowding at Fighter Command knew that something rather special was up. Radar – still known as radio direction-finding, RDF – had detected a swarm of aircraft behind Calais. For weeks following Dunkirk the RAF had waited and wondered when Hitler would lose his temper and attempt to force a quick decision with a vast terror raid on London, but he had not come. As girls of the Women's Auxiliary Air Force, pushing counters with croupier rakes, built up the plots on the operations tables of Fighter Command at Stanmore, of No. 11 Group at Uxbridge and

of No. 11 Group's sector stations it seemed possible that this might be the moment of the great throw.

Even so, Air Vice Marshal Keith Park, the New Zealand leader of No. 11 Group responded cautiously. Two hundred Spitfires and Hurricanes, or about one-third of Britain's first-line fighter defence force were under his command in nineteen squadrons. Six of Spitfires, thirteen of Hurricanes. Park realised that a mistake on his part could lose the war for Britain in a matter of hours. Consequently, as soon as it was appreciated that this was not to be the fateful day, that the target was the channel convoy, the RAF reacted cautiously. Six Hurricanes of No 32 Squadron were already on patrol in the vacinity and a mixed force of twenty more Hurricanes and Spitfires from Nos 11, 74, 64 and 56 Squadrons were ordered up in support.

But the convoy was under attack before even the six patrolling British fighter pilots could reach it and when they did they beheld a daunting and terrifying spectacle. Some seventy Luftwaffe bombers and fighters were smothering the convoy like wasps round a jam jar. To the fighter pilots in the Hurricanes there was no question of awaiting reinforcements. They dived. Six into seventy.

By the time help had arrived, the Hurricanes had obliged the enemy force to spiral itself defensively into a cylinder of three layers above the ships, Me 109s on top, Me 110s in the middle and Do 17 bombers below.

Among the reinforcements were eight Spitfires of No 74 Squadron. Climbing to 13,000 feet, 1,000 feet above the protective Me 109s the Spitfires dived through the cylinder. At sea level most of the Spitfires had spent their ammunition. The convoy sailed on, with the loss of only one small ship. But the Luftwaffe had lost four fighters to the RAF's three. The loss of three fighters in one day might seem of no great concern now that new and repaired Hurricanes and Spitfires were reaching Fighter Command from Beaverbrook's organisation at the rate of more than one hundred aircraft each week. Read in the context, though, of fifteen fighters lost in the preceding seven days, it concerned Dowding. Supposing the Luftwaffe

Air Vice Marshal Keith Park C-in-C No. 11 Group

was to hurl itself against the radar stations, the fighter airfields, the aircraft factories and on London? Then, it was feared, the aggregate of one week's losses in the air, on the ground and in the factories would lay Britain open to invasion.

Hence, the Luftwaffe's July 10 initiative imposed an unhappy dilemma on the defenders of the free world. The alternatives, it seemed, were to let ships at sea take their chance with but a token air cover, and sometimes with none at all, or to risk all over the sea rather than husband fighters and save for the really rainy day. Dowding took the precaution of warning the Navy that convoys might have to fend for themselves.

The sun was still rising on July 11, the second day of the battle, when the dilemma repeated itself and it was Air Fleet 3's turn to test its aim against the ships of a British convoy.

Today von Richthofen's Stuka dive-bombers were to attack a convoy proceeding eastwards across Lyme Bay. Ten Ju 87s escorted by twenty Me 109s of von Richthofen's eager units took off from the neighbourhood of Cherbourg. Radar picked them up. Three Hurricanes of No 501 Squadron from Warmwell in Park's most westerly parish, the Middle Wallop sector of No 11 Group, were ordered forward to engage the enemy, backed by six Spitfires of No 609 Squadron.

The three Hurricane pilots met the

Dover Harbour under attack

Ju 88's: one peeling off to dive *Below:* Coastline ahead

The cost of battle: Crashing Spitfire, *below* Crashed Me 109

uperior Me 109s at odds of nearly 7 to and one Hurricane was quickly shot own. The Spitfires lost two of their umber. One Stuka was destroyed nd the convoy steamed on intact.

On the airfields the young pilots of he fighter squadrons, bursting to get t the enemy with all the zest and mpulsiveness of youth, began to fret. Vhy were those desk-bound fools the rass hats sending them in threes and ixes to meet vastly superior numbers f the enemy when other squadrons, ager to join battle, were being held ack? The pilots of No 609 Squadron ented their feelings on the subject in he squadron operation record book:

'The utter futility of sending very mall sections of fighters to cope with he intense enemy activity in the Portland area is bitterly resented by he pilots. The fact that they have so ften been sent off to make an inter- eption as a section, or possibly a light, only to find themselves hope- essly outnumbered by enemy fighters cting as guard to the bombers, is iscouraging because the British ighter then finds himself unable to do is job of destroying the bombers and s compelled to fight a defensive ction'.

To the British people, unaware that the RAF could muster more than the tiny formations which were apparently fighting a David and Goliath battle with the enemy, every suggestion of uneven odds was meat and drink.

On July 14 as the convoy attacks continued, the nation was treated to a stirring clifftop radio commentary from Dover, which confirmed the popular belief that however inferior the RAF might be numerically, it was more than a match for its mighty adversary. Quality amounted to more than quantity, people reassured them- selves. The radio reporter, Charles Gardner, yelled into a BBC micro- phone, 'Well now, the Germans are dive-bombing a convoy at sea. There are one, two, three, four, five, six, seven German bombers – Junkers eighty-sevens – there's one going down on its target now. Bomb – no, there – he's missed the ships . . . He hasn't got a single ship. There's one coming down with a long streak.

'You can't see these fighters very coherently for long. You just see about four twirling machines and you hear little bursts of machine gun fire, and by the time you've picked up the machine they've gone . . .

'There's a dogfight going on up there – there are four, five, six machines, wheeling and turning round. Hark at the machine guns. Hark, one, two, three, four, five, six . . . Now there's something coming right down on the tail of another. Here they go – yes, they're being chased home and how they're being chased home. There are three Spitfires chasing three Messerschmitts now . . .

'Oh boy! Look at them going. And look how the Messerschmitts – oh that is really grand! And there's a Spitfire just behind the first two – he'll get them!

'Oh, yes – oh boy! I've never seen anything so good as this . . . the RAF fighter boys have really got these boys taped'.

If the continuing air battle which was developing overhead along the coast at the very front door to Britain was something unique in warfare, its capture on disc was equally novel and set off a national controversy. While some argued that it was wrong to broadcast a running commentary of air fighting on the level of a national sporting event, the majority agreed with the general verdict of the press that it was as if the sporting instinct of the British people had come to the cliffs of Dover.

To the perplexed British pilots who were being held back, the broadcast came as a further irritant. 'Why can't we get at them?' was the question running through the messes of squad- ron after squadron.

But at their bases the German pilots were jubilant. From the weak opposition they were encountering it really seemed as though the RAF was almost finished. Certainly, the pilots of the few fighters that harassed them were courageous to the point of fool- hardiness, but their ranks were thin and surely they would not be able to sustain losses.

Allusion to sport was not a British monopoly. At this early stage of the battle Me 109 pilots carried the in- stincts of the chase into their cock- pits; instincts that were encouraged by their commander-in-chief

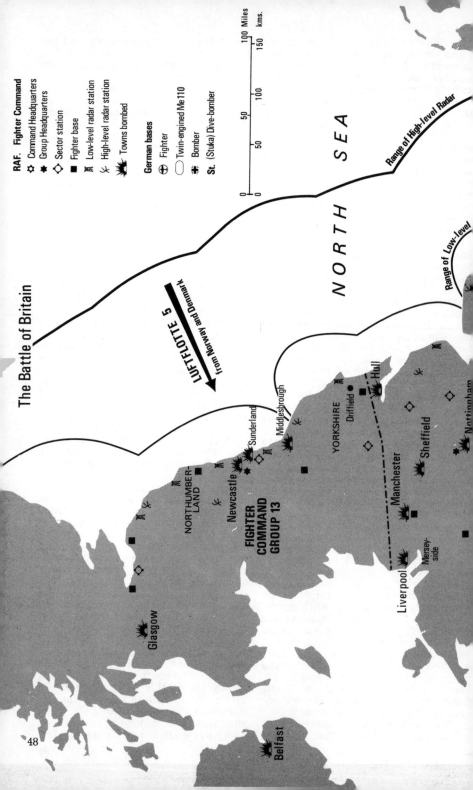

The Battle of Britain

RAF. Fighter Command
- ✧ Command Headquarters
- ★ Group Headquarters
- ★ Sector station
- ◇ Fighter base
- 🏠 Low-level radar station
- 🗲 High-level radar station
- 💥 Towns bombed

German bases
- ⊕ Fighter
- ◯ Twin-engined Me 110
- 🛩 Bomber
- **St.** (Stuka) Dive-bomber

100 Miles
150 kms.

NORTH SEA

Range of High-level Radar

Range of Low-level

LUFTFLOTTE 5
from Norway and Denmark

FIGHTER COMMAND
GROUP 13

Glasgow

Belfast

NORTHUMBER-LAND

Newcastle

Sunderland

Middlesbrough

YORKSHIRE

Driffield

Hull

Manchester

Sheffield

Liverpool

Mersey-side

Nottingham

48

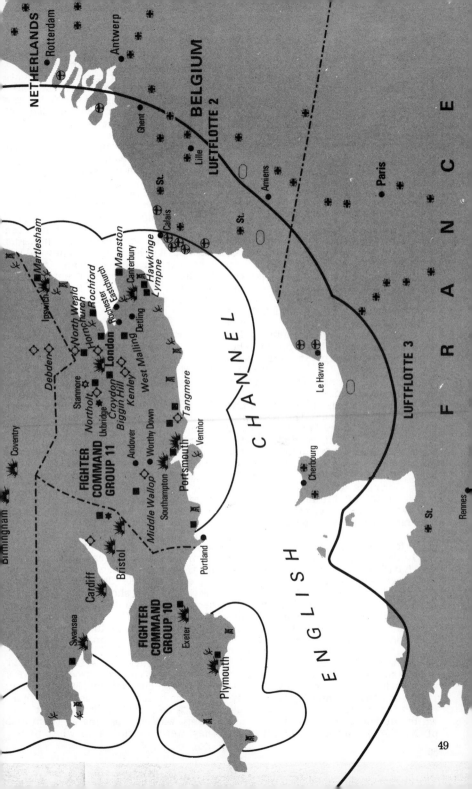

Hermann Goering who invited top-scoring fighter aces to relax at his hunting lodge in Prussia.

Such invitations were not, however, always as welcome as the Reich Marshal believed. Not because the pilots were squeamish about shooting a royal stag but because they feared that in their short absence from the front their individual scores would be bettered. Thus, when Werner Molders, summoned by Goering following his fortieth kill, was taking his leave after three days, the pilot persuaded the Reich Marshal to detain his successor Adolf Galland for an equal period.

However, in spite of the odds in their favour as the battle opened, German pilots very soon learned to temper keeness with caution. Galland has explained in his book 'The First and The Last':

'Any encounter with British fighters called for maximum effort . . . I can only express the highest admiration for the British fighter pilots who, although technically at a disadvantage fought bravely and indefatigably. They undoubtedly saved their country in this crucial hour'.

The technical disadvantage as the battle began was that the RAF possessed many more of the slower Hurricanes and Spitfires and even the Spitfire was not a fair match for the Me 109 in July 1940. As Winston Churchill summed the aircraft up, 'The Germans were faster with a better rate of climb; ours more manoeuverable, better armed'.

In fact, despite the disparity of the numbers in combat, the score, aircraft for aircraft, was going against the Luftwaffe. In the first nine days of the Battle of Britain, the Germans lost sixty-one aircraft to Fighter Command's twenty-eight. And then, on the tenth day of the fighting, the first of what was to become an accumulating sum of disasters hit the RAF, one squadron losing six out of eight Defiant fighters destroyed to the Luftwaffe's two on July 19.

To describe the Defiant as a fighter aircraft is factually correct, but the turret-gunned, dumpy Defiant aircraft of Nos 141 and 264 Squadrons, while not being obsolete in the sense of No 247 Squadron's Gladiator bi-planes, stationed near Plymouth in the west country, were obvious misfits among Hurricanes and Spitfires.

Eager as their more fortunate comrades in the single-seater-squadrons to get into the fight, the pilots and air-gunners of No 141 Squadron were jubilant when they were ordered south from Scotland. Their elation was not unfounded, for the Defiant had earlier enjoyed a peak day of glory in combat with Stukas over Dunkirk.

On the morning of July 19 nine Defiant aircraft flew forward from West Malling to the coastal airfield of Hawkinge. Shortly before lunch the order came. Patrol at five thousand feet south of Folkestone. They did not last long. Out of the sun and from ten thousand feet above them twenty Me 109s dived on the dawdling Defiants. In moments five Defiant aircraft had plunged into the sea. A sixth crashed on the coast.

Next morning seven new Defiant fighters flew in to join the Squadron – true to Beaverbrook's promise to Fighter Command, to replace losses as they occurred. The following day, two weeks after No 141 Squadron had flown down from Scotland so eagerly, the Squadron was returned to the north leaving six aircraft behind. There were no airmen to crew them.

As the July days passed, such incidents as the destruction of the Defiants falsely encouraged Luftwaffe crews that the RAF was being reduced beyond recovery. They were further heartened by encountering Spitfires and Hurricanes in such small numbers. Moreover, there was also a rewarding daylight reduction of British shipping from the channel areas under attack. If this maritime power could be driven from the Channel with such despatch, then should invasion prove necessary it would very likely take place unopposed!

None of the grimness of their position was lost on the defenders during these warm July days. By the evening of July 23 the Luftwaffe had lost eighty-five aircraft to the RAF's forty-five, but neither Dowding nor Park held any illusions about their predicament. They knew that the enemy was only pawing at them and they were fearful as to what might

Boulton Paul 'Defiant'

Ju 87 'Stuka'. Both planes were
virtually obsolete before the battle

befall Fighter Command were the enemy to capitalise on his full resources. It was getting that the Luftwaffe had temporarily deprived the Royal Navy of command of the Channel, a humiliation that was heightened by the events of July 25.

Following a day of simultaneous Air Fleet 2 attacks on convoys in the Thames Estuary and the Straits of Dover, sixty bombers escorted by fighters harried a convoy of twenty-one merchant ships, the majority of which were colliers. Five ships were quickly sent to the bottom and six more were crippled in a series of ferocious and accurate dive-bomber attacks. To drive home the message that Germany was challenging England for permanent command of the Channel, a flotilla of E-boats put to sea in broad daylight. The E-boats were at sea again during the night and finished off three of the crippled ships.

Further humiliation followed on July 27 when the Luftwaffe sank two destroyers from Dover and damaged a third. After a third destroyer had been sunk on July 29, the Dover destroyers were withdrawn to the relative and temporary safety of Portsmouth.

Air superiority first over the Channel and second over south-east England, was the German prerequisite of peace with or without invasion and the High Command was greatly encouraged by the results of the Luftwaffe's exploratory operations. But, whereas the RAF reckoned that its battle for Britain had begun, the Luftwaffe was still on a tight rein and impatient to intensify operations.

On July 30 Hitler personally instructed Goering to put the Luftwaffe in a state of immediate readiness for the great onslaught, the 'attack of the eagles' as the German staff planners knew it. The Luftwaffe, Hitler directed, was to stand-by 'to destroy the flying units, ground organisations and supply installations of the RAF and the British air armaments industry'.

Hitler now had only to whisper the code word 'Eagle Day' to initiate an attack new in the history of warfare, a sustained air assault upon the mother country of a world imperial power.

In Britain people were blissfully unaware of Hitler's directive. Life in London was astonishingly tranquil considering the peril in which the capital lay. On August 3 the RAF fielded an eleven for a friendly game of cricket against the London Fire Service at Lords Cricket ground. On the same day the British Overseas Airways flying-boat Clare, made the first British passenger service flight to the new world. It was a milestone and an indication that the Atlantic would not quarantine the new world from European infection very much longer.

By August 8 when Clare was returning with a party of American pilots engaged by the Ministry of Aircraft Production to ferry new and repaired aircraft from factory to airfield, Goering and his Luftwaffe commanders were meeting at Karinhall to complete plans for the attack of the eagles. Over the brandy and cigars and playing toy railways in the Karinhall atmosphere of make-believe, Goering and his Air Fleet leaders persuaded themselves that given four days of good weather the Luftwaffe could gain air superiority over southeast England and win the war for Germany. Certainly, the Luftwaffe's prowess in the Channel operations of August 8 seemed to support this confident outlook.

In the early hours of August 8 the Royal Navy sent a convoy of twenty-five merchant ships into the straits of Dover, hoping to slip the convoy through the dangerous narrows under cover of darkness. Since the convoy attacks of July the Royal Navy had considerably strengthened convoy defences. This convoy of twenty-five merchant ships was accompanied by barrage balloon vessels and anti-aircraft destroyers.

But the enemy had also been busy since early July and had built a radar station at Wissant across the water from Dover, a move of which the Admiralty was unaware as it attempted to slip the convoy through the straits and into more open sea.

Out from their lairs along the French coast streaked a force of fast torpedo-firing E-boats. They sank three ships and damaged two more before dawn. Later in the day the remainder of the convoy was sailing in the neighbourhood of the Isle of Wight when the Luftwaffe found it.

The Stuka dive-bombers came in twice, in formations of more than eighty 'and fifty at a time' and each Ju 87 formation was escorted by about three times as many fighters. It was an open challenge to Fighter Command – 'come up and fight and protect your ships', the type of challenge the Luftwaffe was confident would reduce the RAF's numbers of Spitfires and Hurricanes, and hasten the end of the war.

Seven Squadrons were scrambled from 10 and 11 Groups. To Squadron Leader JRA Peel leading No 1 Squadron of Hurricanes, the Stuka seemed like a swarm of little black dots as the British fighters dive. Larger and larger the dots grew unt each enlarged into the vulture-lik outline of a Stuka, the Ju 87 div bomber.

'Look out, 109s!' The Hurrican pilots in the moment of pouncing o their slow, defenceless prey, wer themselves in the gunsights of Germa fighters. The hunters had become th hunted. Stepped up in the sun th Me 109 pilots, the guardian angels c the vulnerable Stukas, had seen wha was about to happen. In seconds the were on the tails of the Hurricane forcing the RAF pilots to break o and defend themselves. Squadro Leader Peel, jumped by two Me 109 reported 'The enemy fighters wer half-rolling and diving and zoon ing in climbing turns. I fired two five seconds' bursts at one and saw i dive into the sea. Then I followe another up in a zoom and got him a he stalled'. But they got Peel. H came down in the sea close to th enemy coast at Boulogne. When rescu boats reported they would probabl have to turn back, Peel's Squadro signalled, 'Tell the boats they'll b shot up by us if they do'. The Squadro Leader was rescued.

In the furious fighting of August Hurricanes and Spitfires accounte for thirty-one of the enemy for a los of nineteen of their number, figure exceeding those of any single day' fighting since July 10. The convo sailed on but not without losing si ships to the E-boats and dive-bombers

The battle was warming up for bot sides and excitement and confidenc were rising in the British cockpit now that the pilots were bein gradually committed in large numbers. There was a new earnest ness, too. Death, disfigurement b burning, and all the wounds of ai fighting among the fighter squadrons were bringing it home to the youn pilots in their late 'teens and earl twenties – as a general rule Dowdin believed fighter squadron comman ders should not top twenty-six – tha they were engaged in a business vastl more serious than a great game o ven the sport of Charles Gardner's broadcast commentary. Any remaining air of unreality was now to be found on the ground, among people whose sporting instincts it would take more than Hitler to deny.

Traditionally, grouse shooting began on August 12. It was war work of national importance the British Broadcasting Corporation explained and King George VI generously presented game shot on his estates to military hospitals rather than to members of his family as was the peacetime custom.

The significance of August 12 in the British sporting calendar was not lost on the Luftwaffe which admitted to the 'Nazi caddishness' of bagging ninety RAF planes on the wrong day – August 11.

The Luftwaffe's arithmetic was as faulty as its knowledge of British tradition was correct. It had lost thirty-eight aircraft to the RAF's thirty-two. Nevertheless, RAF losses reflected the rising cost of the increased committal of fighters to the battle.

On August 12, meteorological reports indicated that the weather was improving and that on the morrow conditions might justify the issue of the long awaited code signal, 'Eagle Day!' Certainly, August 12 dawned fine and clear, excepting occasional patches of mist and as the season's first birds were falling to the guns on the British moors, the Luftwaffe employed the improved weather to make a new move. For the first time in the battle it tried to destroy Dowding's coastal radar warning stations and the front line airfields of the defence control system they served.

The effectiveness of this system owed everything to Dowding's dogged pre-war insistence upon tight communications, in short, true control. However, while the fount of all instructions was to be found at Fighter Command headquarters, many of the most critical decisions during the battle were taken at the headquarters of Air Vice Marshal Park's No 11 Group which bore the brunt of the attack.

No-one could visit No 11 Group at Uxbridge in 1940 without carrying away an indelible impression and Winston Churchill was no exception! 'The Group Operations Room was like a small theatre, about sixty feet across, and with two storeys. We took our seats in the Dress Circle. Below us was the large-scale map table, around which perhaps twenty highly-trained young men and women, with their telephone assistants, were assembled. Opposite to us, covering the entire wall, where the theatre curtain would be, was a gigantic blackboard divided into six columns with electric bulbs, for the six fighter stations, each of their squadrons having a sub-column of its own, and also divided by lateral lines. Thus the lowest row of bulbs showed as they were lighted the squadrons which were 'Standing By' at two minutes' notice, the next row those at 'Readiness', five minutes, then at 'Available', twenty minutes, then those which had taken off, the next row those which had reported having seen the enemy, the next – with red lights – those which were in action, and the top row those which were returning home. On the left-hand side, in a kind of glass stage-box, were the four or five officers whose duty it was to weigh and measure the information received from our Observer Corps, which at this time numbered upwards of fifty thousand men, women and youths. Radar was still in its infancy but it gave warning of raids approaching our coast, and the observers, with field-glasses and portable telephones, were our main source of information about raiders flying overland. Thousands of messages were therefore received during an action. Several roomfuls of experienced people in other parts of the underground headquarters sifted them with great rapidity, and transmitted the results from minute to minute directly to the plotters seated around the table on the floor and to the officer supervising from the glass stage-box. 'On the right hand was another glass stage-box containing Army officers who reported the action of our anti-aircraft batteries * . . .'

It had taken the Air Fleet commanders, Kesselring and Sperrle, some weeks to appreciate the full signifi-

* 'Their Finest Hour' by Winston S. Churchill: Houghton Mifflin

Pilot Officer BE 'Paddy' Finucane

Portsmouth Harbour under attack

54

cance of the tall radar masts – the eyes of this system – which the Graf Zeppelin had so inadequately investigated and even now the air fleets were uncertain as to the accuracy of Dowding's radar in assisting interception. But they suspected that if the attack of the eagles was to eliminate fighter resistance in the south of England in four days, then the Luftwaffe must liquidate first the radar eyes and second the forward airfields of the enemy squadrons. After early morning feint attacks across the Dover straits before breakfast on August 12 the Luftwaffe delivered its first heavyweight blows against Dowding's defence system.

By nine o'clock the vital south coast chain of radar sites was under attack, bombers and fighters hurling themselves at six stations between Dover and the Isle of Wight where the Ventnor station was put off the air. The Luftwaffe swept down, too, on the Kent coastal fighter fields of Manston, Hawkinge and Lympne. Situated on the very coastline, these airfields were extremely vulnerable. No 65 Squadron of Spitfires, after flying forward from Rochford was still on the ground when the first of one hundred and seventy-five bombs began to fall on Manston. In the melee as the Spitfires raced across the airfield to get airborne was Pilot Officer BE 'Paddy' Finucane, who had recently joined the Squadron. Already that morning he had been in action in a Squadron mix-up with thirty Me 109s over the sea. Then, evading attack by two persistent Me 109 pilots, Finucane climbed to thirty thousand feet and sighted twelve more enemy aircraft. He reported, 'I dived into the foremost aircraft. It went into the sea, grey smoke pouring from it'. Now over Manston the Pilot Officer bagged another Me 109. He was on his way towards a credit of thirty-two victories and promotion to Wing Commander.

Manston, Hawkinge and Lympne suffered badly from the raids. At Hawkinge, Ju 88s wrecked two hangars, destroyed the workshops and pitted the airfield.

Fortunately for the defenders the attacks on the radar stations and forward airfields were about the sum total of the Luftwaffe's attention on August 12 to the truly tactical targets. It was with relief that Dowding observed the weight of attack being transferred to two convoys in the Thames Estuary and, westwards, to the naval base at Portsmouth.

Here, one of the boldest raids of the Battle of Britain took place. Flying through the narrow harbour entrance to take advantage of a gap in the pattern of barrage balloons, came a force of Stuka dive-bombers. Luckily, for an area brimming with worthwhile targets, little naval or military damage was caused. 'There was about everything of which an airman dreams' a German pilot broadcast after the raid. 'Enormous ships lay at anchor and in the docks. The targets were so close together it was hardly possible to miss them'. But they did. Their bombs hit a brewery, an achievement which, while no doubt damaging to naval morale, would not win the war for Germany.

At the end of the day when the RAF was wondering how long it could hold out if the Luftwaffe were to concentrate its full resources against the radar stations and fighter airfields, Luftwaffe staff and aircrew were congratulating themselves on a battle already almost won. They simply erased the attacked targets from their maps and claimed some sixty fighters destroyed.

In truth, the Luftwaffe had lost thirty-one aircraft to the RAF twenty-two. Manston was out of action until the next day, and work had already started to replace the Ventnor radar station at nearby Bembridge.

The eagle swoops

When at long last it came, when after all the procrastination the code name was passed on August 13, the attack of the eagles was something of an anticlimax and in its first moments almost a fiasco. Not that the defenders noticed or appreciated this at the time. They feared that the unprecedented attacks on the mainland the previous day must herald heavier and heavier blows, possibly invasion. But the Luftwaffe bungled its opportunity at the start. Shortly after the launch, Eagle Day was hastily cancelled, but the change of orders failed to reach all units briefed to attack.

For this bonus the defenders could thank the changeability of the British weather. Tuesday, August 13, was born a dull day. Visibility was poor over the Luftwaffe bases in France and the low countries, and the morning was cloudy in southern England. However, if Britain was to be broken before winter, Eagle Day was already hazardously late. Thus, when the meteorological forecast compiled from air reconnaissance, U-Boat messages and the broken cipher of Britain's radioed Atlantic weather information,

seemed promising enough, the attack of the eagles was signalled. By the time the actual state of the weather over England became known, Goering's personal decision to postpone operations until the afternoon reached parts of the Air Fleets too late.

For ground crews and air crews in both the Luftwaffe and the RAF Eagle Day brought an early start. By 5.30 am more than seventy Dornier 17s were airborne.

Had Colonel Fink, commanding the Dorniers received the High Command's cancellation, he and his men could have enjoyed another hour or two in their beds. But, the early morning of August 13 found them gathering over their bases, anxiously searching for the large fighter escort which was scheduled to join them. But the cancellation which had failed to reach Fink had been received by the fighters shortly after becoming airborne. They were not, however, in radio communication with the bombers they were supposed to shepherd to their targets and home again. So concerned was the fighter leader about his charges that, clowning aerobatically,

Bomber strike: Do 17's over Britain

e tried to attract Fink's attention.
but in vain. The fighters had their
rders to return to base. The bombers
ad their orders to launch the attack
f the Eagles and orders were to be
beyed. Cancellation was radioed
esperately from Kesselring's head-
uarters but Fink's receiver was out
f order. The message was picked up
n another bomber but misunderstood
s confirming that the raid was on.

Thus Fink found himself leading the
rst mission of Eagle Day inexplicably
eserted by his fighter escort. But his
uck was not entirely out because the
reat bank of cloud which had in-
pired the official postponement of the
ttack so confused the RAF's radar
efences and the ground Observer
orps whose task it was to pass eye-
ight reports of enemy formations to
ighter controllers, that his bomber
orce was assured a milk run.

The bombers' navigation was ex-
ellent for there, ten thousand feet
below, and at the very moment that
he heavy clouds began to break up,
ay Eastchurch airfield. Luftwaffe

bomb aimers could see RAF planes
paraded as though ready for a public
open-day on a peacetime station.

It was a wasteful target, as it
happened, because Eastchurch was a
Coastal Command aerodrome and not
one of Fighter Command's regular
sector stations. Yet, if the Luftwaffe
was out to reduce the RAF's fighter
strength in the air, an attack here was
as likely to draw Dowding's fighters
to the defence as an attack anywhere
along the invasion front of southern
England; a plus that was negated in
this instance by the absence of German
fighters.

Fink's bombs were falling at 7 am
when the defenders, poorly alerted
because of the cloudy weather and an
unusually weak radar plot, realised
that Eastchurch was being attacked.
It now remained to intercept the
'bandits' on their way home and
fortunately Squadron Leader John
Thompson patrolling No 111 Squadron's
Hurricanes over Folkestone was already nicely positioned for the job.
The Hurricanes tore into the Dorniers
and, making a meal of them, shot
down five enemy aircraft within as

Ack-ack fire

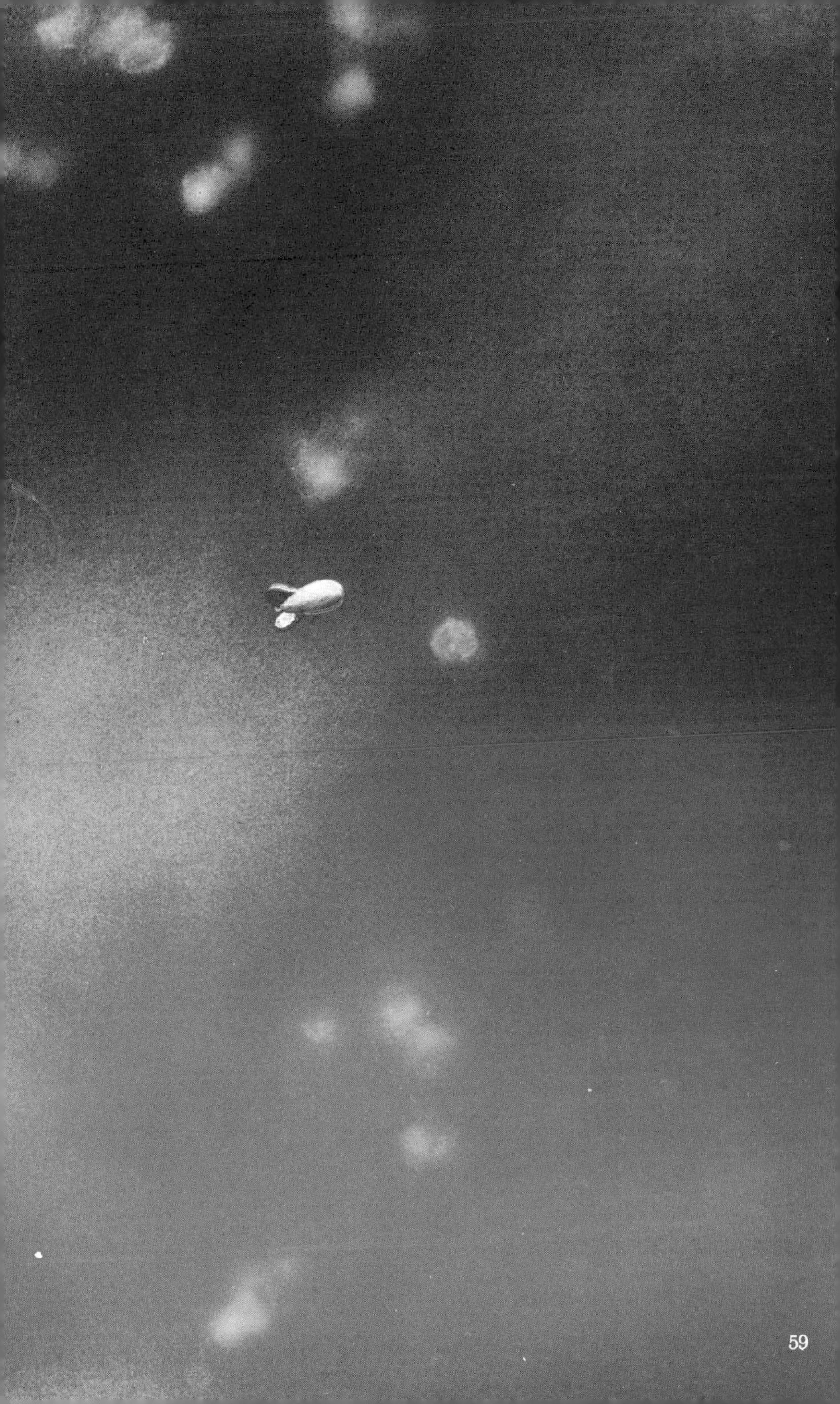

Sqd Ldr 'Sailor' Malan
Right: Ju 88's

many minutes. About half an hour afterwards Thompson and his pilots were taking a second breakfast in the mess at Croydon.

Fink's force, now broken up and desperately anxious to get home, cursed the absence of the fighters which had failed to accompany him on the outward flight. Not only had the Luftwaffe bombers been exposed to the full fury of No 111 Squadron's attack but they had also been blasted over the Whitstable oyster beds by more Hurricanes from No 151 Squadron and Spitfires from the South African ace, Squadron Leader 'Sailor' Malan's No 74 Squadron.

Fink, himself, reached base safely but at the age of fifty and with a paternal sense of responsibility for his young crews, he was not an officer to write-off the experience in gratitude for the safety of his own skin. He complained bitterly to his Air Fleet Commander, Kesselring, who understanding a senior subordinate's outburst in the circumstances, personally explained and apologised for the mistake.

While the Dorniers, for all the bad management at base, had succeeded in finding the relatively unimportant target at Eastchurch, a force of escorted Ju 88 bombers, operating to the west, was completely foxed by the cloudy weather. Splitting into two sections the Ju 88s were seeking the fighter field at Odiham and the RAF's research and development establishment at Farnborough – targets which, like the Coastal Command field at Eastchurch, did not rate the flattering

attention of the Luftwaffe's attack of the eagles. Destruction of the Odiham and Farnborough stations even if it had taken place would not have contributed towards the four day victory on which Goering was counting. Unfortunately for the Ju 88s not only were they unable to find the two airfields, but they also ran into No's 43, 64 and 601 Squadrons in the course of their search.

One of No 601s pilots was an American volunteer, Pilot Officer Billy Fiske. Scrambled from Tangmere at 0645 hours for the first of several sorties on August 13, Fiske in his RAF blue uniform had no need to be seeking trouble in the skies over Britain before breakfast. His country was neutral and its volunteer Eagle Squadron was not to become operational until after the Battle of Britain. In the early morning fighting Fiske was credited with one Ju 88 probably destroyed and a second German bomber damaged.

Later in the morning of August 13 the Luftwaffe again bungled the attack of the eagles. In this case, a reverse of error which had so upset the Dornier crews before breakfast, an Air Fleet 3 bomber force failed to rendez-vous with its fighters for a mid-morning raid on the naval base at Portland. The fighters, an intended bomber escort of some thirty Me 110 'destroyer' fighters, were routed. Five Me 110s were shot down in six minutes and the remainder turned tail and fled for the safety of France.

One of the RAF pilots, a British baronet, Flight Lieutenant Sir Archibald Hope of No 601 Squadron reported, characteristically, 'I fired a short burst at one enemy aircraft head-on and as I passed I took another the same way. He tightened his turn and pulled straight up across me so that I could see all his pale blue underneath. I finished my bullets into his bottom . . .'

With good radar notice two Squadrons from 10 Group and one of Park's Squadrons had operated as a wing in this action rather than in the more customary smaller numbers. Although encountering the already discredited Me 110, the three Squadrons, accustomed to fighting at odds, were greatly encouraged by the enemy's headlong flight from superior numbers of British fighters.

After this action it was again, as it so often seemed to the fighter pilots that summer, so quiet and lonely over the sea. The sky trail scars had healed, but it was not necessarily time to go home. Over the sea, activity often continued while fuel remained. This day, Flight Lieutenant Hope of 601 Squadron let down to look for friends who might be 'in the drink'. He knew that lives were being saved daily by the care fighter pilots were taking to locate and protect their comrades in the sea. Hope reported, 'I am convinced that unless we had circled these pilots in the water they would not have been picked up. They were easy to see from the air as long as their parachutes were floating, ie for half an hour at most'. The Flight Lieutenant spotted one of his own pilots, directed a naval motor torpedo boat to the rescue and a life was saved. The pilot was picked up, taken to the naval hospital at Portland to have his shrapnel wounds dressed, and late that night had returned to his Squadron at Tangmere.

That, failing the loyalty of his fellows, an operationally-experienced fighter pilot might have been drowned without rescue being attempted, reflected the sad lack of a practised Air-Sea Rescue Service in August, 1940. As the battle began there were only fourteen high speed RAF launches for air-sea rescue around the long coastline of Britain.

The lives of fighter pilots were at a high premium. Although volunteers in the lifeboats of the Royal National Lifeboat Institution were doing their courageous best and seaside amateurs were helping too, the sea was taking its toll of men who ought to have been saved.

One rescue was made by a young woman civilian putting out to sea in a small and fragile canoe and paddling back with a pilot. The King gave her a medal.

Such an exploit was inspiring and in

Down in the Drink: Stages in a rescue
Top: Patrolling 'Lysander' spots baled -out pilot
Middle: Air Sea Rescue launch en route
Bottom: In friendly hands again

keeping with the spirit of 1940 but it also illuminated the need for a crash emergency air-sea rescue scheme. Hastily the RAF, the Navy and the Army, combined to form a channel rescue service, comprising RAF launches, light naval craft and twelve Lysander spotter aircraft borrowed from the Army to drop dinghies.

In contrast, Germany had a well-planned service for fishing airmen out of the channel and returning them to active service. The Luftwaffe was equipped with He 59 float planes and fast launches. As the battle developed it introduced a luxury sea rescue float fitted with four bunks, blankets, clothing, food and water and stationed at intervals in the middle of the channel.

While Me 109 pilots carried inflatable dinghies, Hurricane and Spitfire pilots were dependent solely upon their 'Mae Wests'. There was, however, one feature of the British rescue arrangements with which the Luftwaffe could not compete and this was the Royal Air Force Pigeon Service which had been established before the war.

Despite continuing bad weather the Luftwaffe resumed operations in the afternoon of August 13. The great banks of heavy, low cloud rolling across the south of England were certainly not conducive to the open-skied fighter actions which the Luftwaffe confidently expected would rub out the RAF fighter force.

Nevertheless, the Luftwaffe intensified its effort after lunch, parading fighters, bombers and dive-bombers from the Thames estuary in the east to Southampton in the west.

Ninety heavily escorted bombers were sent. The intention was to extend the southern fighter defences to the limit, knock out a number of airfields and give the docks at Southampton a bad time in passing. It was, of course, the sort of tall order that could only have originated in the euphoric atmosphere of Karinhall.

Altogether the plan met with a very sketchy success. True, a force of Ju 88 bombers got through to Southampton and started serious fires in the docks but no airfields of importance were damaged and the Luftwaffe fared disappointingly wherever breaks in the cloud gave intercepting Squadrons an opportunity to do battle.

One 10 Group Squadron in which Pilot Officers Andy Mamedoff, Re[d] Tobin and Shorty Keogh, three of the American Bill Fiske's volunteer compatriots were serving, did remarkably well and made the following exhilarating report: 'Thirteen Spitfires left Warmwell for a memorable tea-time party over Lyme Bay and an unlucky day for the species of Ju 87 in which no less than fourteen suffered destruction or damage in a record Squadron bag, which also included five of the escorting Mes.

'The enemy's formation, consisting of about forty dive-bombers in 4 Vic formation, with about as many Me 110s and 109s stepped up above them, heading northwards from the Channel, was surprised by 609 Squadron's down-sun attack. All thirteen of our pilots fired their guns . . .' One British fighter pilot, who on the previous day had been bemoaning his unavoidable absence from the grouse moors on the 'Glorious Twelfth', reckoned that 609 Squadron's success on the thirteenth had more than compensated for the disappointment.

During the afternoon the RAF was kept busy, too, on its eastern and more vulnerable flank. Here again the Luftwaffe selected a target of secondary importance, attacking Detling which, as with Eastchurch in the morning, was primarily a Coastal Command station. Although the station commander was killed in a dive-bombing attack and the operations room, messes and cookhouse all destroyed, the station cleared up the mess and had essential services running by the lunch hour next day.

In the late afternoon the attack of the eagles, the day that was to see the beginning of the end of Fighter Command, fizzled out. At sunset the Luftwaffe had flown one thousand four hundred and eighty-five sorties, about one-third of them by bombers, to the RAF's seven hundred. In the post-war count it was learned that the Luftwaffe had lost forty-five aircraft to the RAF's unlucky thirteen. At the time, however, the Luftwaffe believed it had done well. Claiming destruction of eighty-eight British fighters under adverse weather conditions it gave itself good reason to see

scramble!

the end in sight.

As if to add omen to German confidence there was a report the next morning that during the last moments of August 13, Big Ben had struck not twelve but thirteen sonorous notes at the midnight hour.

The Royal Air Force – despite its air success on August 13, held no illusions about the extreme peril of its situation. The increased volume and more widespread nature of the Luftwaffe's August 13 action had stretched the front line Squadrons now that larger numbers of Hurricanes and Spitfires were being committed against the bigger enemy formations.

Comparatively, August 14 was quieter and yet as a successor to the broader scope of the previous day's operations the defenders found it taxing enough. Even though the Luftwaffe was blunting the effect of its own operations by flying in poor weather and selecting relatively unrewarding targets, it nevertheless held the advantage of surprise. Radar

supplemented by visual reports from the Observer Corps could serve Dowding and his group commanders with a reasonable accuracy but the very diversity of the Luftwaffe's attacks and its generally curious choice of targets served to confuse the deployment of the defending Squadrons along a two hundred and fifty mile coastal front. It still remained to be seen if Fighter Command could sustain the all out blow which had been so long expected and feared since the fall of France. On August 15 the true test began, when the first, and as it transpired, the only time in the course of the battle the Luftwaffe hurled three Air Fleets at Britain.

This was to be the day of the big throw, the true attack of the eagles, the first of four days in which the RAF would be driven from the skies of southern England. Attack, attack, attack, along a wide front from the east coast to the west coast of England. Finish off the radar stations, wreck the aerodromes, force the remaining fighters up to do battle and destroy them.

August 15 was the day for which

German armchair strategists had waited impatiently as they gloated over the press maps, diagrams and cartoons which projected an encircled England, the German eagle at her throat. The German radio – broadcasting in English so that the enemy be in no doubt of his approaching fate – brashly announced, 'England lies on a salver awaiting the German Air Force's attack. She cannot escape. John Bull will be smoked out. Either he will surrender or England will be annihilated'.

As dawn spread across the British Isles, enemy activity was restricted to routine reconnaissance flight. Even the morning raids on the forward airfields at Lympne and Hawkinge, severe though they were, could be accounted fairly normal in the circumstances. As valuable to the enemy, however, were the feint attacks which failed to materialise. From dawn the Luftwaffe kept the Squadrons of 11 Group on their toes. The wear and tear on men and machines was already beginning to tell and the repeated take-offs and landings increased the danger of Squadrons being caught rearming and refuelling on the ground. Here, the basic problem was that responsibility for the defence of south-east England, the invasion area, and of London, lay mainly with fighter stations built into a defence system which had presumed that enemy bomber bases were comfortably beyond the Meuse. Not only were the most forward airfields exposed to sudden attack but pilots operating from them were often obliged to climb inland to reach an altitude from which to return and fight.

Thus, until midday several sharp airfield attacks in south-east England and many Channel feints kept 11 Group busy and guessing, while, in the north of England, hitherto a quiet sector, a novel situation was developing.

For some while, German airmen of Stumpff's Air Fleet 5 based in occupied Norway and Denmark had coveted the more active, more glorious role of their comrades in Air Fleets 2 and 3. Now, they were to receive their opportunity to take a hand in the imminent defeat of the Royal Air Force, and as they taxied for take-off they believed a joyride lay ahead them. For Stumpff's orders were destroy airfields in north-east Engla and in Yorkshire in the belief th fighter defences in the north and t midlands had been drained to reinfor the invasion front.

But German intelligence was wron The only switching of Squadro from quiet sectors to the batt sectors had been as between tired a rested Squadrons. In the Royal Flyi Corps, as a mere junior officer, Dow ing had seen exhausted pilots sent to die over the trenches of the fir world war. He was not the man repeat this error of his 1914-19 superiors unless faced with no alte native. The eager crews of Air Fleet were in for an unpleasant surprise.

Soon after noon Fighter Comma learned that enemy aircraft were o hundred miles out to sea from t Firth of Forth on the east coast Scotland. This excellent warning, much better than that which No Group's Squadrons in south-ea England could normally expect, e abled Air Vice Marshal RE Sau No 13 Group to scramble fighters good time to meet the enemy ov the sea.

The fact that east coast radar, more accurate in the estimate numbers than the busier and mo practised south coast chain, unde estimated the enemy force of som sixty-five He 111 bombers and thirt four Me 110 long-range fighters, was no matter. Saul sent up every one his serviceable aircraft – three Squa rons of Spitfires, one of Hurrican and even one squadron of Blenheim aircraft which, while part of the ord of battle of Fighter Command, shou hardly be mentioned in the sam context as the 72 Squadron's Spitfire streaking out to sea to engage t enemy.

Thirty miles out, beyond the blea Farne Islands, the Spitfire pilo spotted the enemy, and it was a sig both tantalising and awe-inspirir that greeted the British fighter pilot Radar had forecast a force of som thirty plus but there, below then

Rearming. Browning 303 ammunition being fed into housings
Above: Hurricane. *Below:* Spitfire

were – as the pilots quickly calculated – one hundred unescorted bombers. In round figures their arithmetic was correct but the RAF pilots had wrongly identified the Me 110 long-range fighter escort carrying large extra fuel tanks for the long haul from Scandinavia. Momentarily, the Spitfire leader, Flight Lieutenant Edward Graham, stopped mentally in his tracks. It was as if a child had been presented with an outsize piece of birthday cake and could not decide where to begin. He was staggered at the sight of the enemy in such numbers. In seconds, though, indecision and wonder gave way to action. Graham and his Squadron tore into the enemy with gluttony of men who have long been hungry for just such an opportunity.

Given an advantage usually denied their comrades in the south of England where the sea crossing was so short, the Spitfire pilots had out-climbed the incoming force during their flight of interception. Now, three thousand feet above the German crews, and with the sun ideally behind their necks, the British fighter pilots dived into the massed Heinkels and Messerschmitts.

In the fight that followed, the fighter escort of Me 110s fared worse than the bombers. Without their air-gunners, who had been left behind in Norway and Denmark because of the long-range nature of the operation, some pilots of Goering's discredited 'destroyer' fighter, jettisoned their fuel tanks and formed a defensive circle. Others put their noses down to the waves and unashamedly raced for home.

The Heinkels with their longer range and showing more determination, broke up into two groups and crossed the coast. Harried by Saul's supporting Squadrons they were unable to reach their target airfields and returned with a loss of eight of their number to Stavanger in Norway. With the additional loss of seven fighters to the RAF's nil it had been a costly daylight initiation for Stumpff's Air Fleet 5 men who had set off so confidently.

But one hundred miles to the south an Air Fleet 5 force of fifty of the faster, more agile Ju 88s was meeting with better fortune. Sweeping across the north sea from Aalborg in northern Denmark, the Junkers bombers were reported by east coast radar and became the responsibility of Air Vice Marshal Trafford Leigh-Mallory's No 12 Group. Operating in sectors south of Saul's Squadrons, and consequently already more generally involved in the Battle of Britain than their northern neighbours, Leigh-Mallory's Squadrons were nevertheless still seeking the opportunities which would soon come their way as the battle over south-east England was carried to London.

Now, as an appetizer, the unescorted Ju 88s approaching Flamborough Head offered themselves to twelve Spitfire pilots of No 616 Squadron and six Hurricane pilots from No 73 Squadron who between them accounted for the destruction of eight bombers. Heavily engaged, the Junkers split up but a force of about thirty bombers made a determined attack on an RAF bomber station at Great Driffield in Yorkshire. The damage was extensive and ten Whitley bombers were destroyed on the ground. This was a serious loss for the RAF though happily for the defenders, Air Fleet 5 had selected a *bomber* station. The equivalent havoc at a fighter field would have been of far greater value to the Luftwaffe, at this stage of the battle. Such an attempt to interrupt the RAF's pin-prick bomber effort of the period, was wasteful so long as Fighter Command the key to the front door to England remained in being. For this valiant if profligate effort, the Luftwaffe paid the sum of eight Ju 88 bombers. Losing twenty-three aircraft out of one hundred and twenty-three serviceable bombers and thirty-four fighters, Air Fleet 5 called it a day after August 15 and were not to re-appear before nightfall in any numbers for the remainder of the battle.

In the south, where large scale daylight attacks by Air Fleets 2 and 3 had no longer the novelty of Air Fleet 5's once-and-for-all day trip across the north sea, the events of August 15 were more testing for the defenders. Here, the hand the defenders had so long expected and feared was being played, as the whole fury of two Air Fleets was hurled gainst Dowding's frontline fighter irfields.

In mid-morning forty Ju 87 dive-ombers, escorted by sixty fighters ttacked the forward airfields at ,ympne and Hawkinge. Lympne was evastated and rendered unusable for wo days. Hawkinge was not so badly amaged but more serious was the hutting down of two radar links in he chain because of a power failure.

One hour later twelve Me 109s dived n the clifftop aerodrome at Manston, aking it with cannon and machine-un fire and destroying two Spitfires n the ground. By three o'clock in the fternoon it was the turn of the more nland fighter station at Martlesham leath to sustain a savage dive-ombing attack by a force of strongly scorted Stukas. Simultaneously one undred Luftwaffe fighters and ombers were approaching the Kent oast followed half an hour later by nother force of one hundred and fifty ircraft.

This was it. Any thoughts of hoard-ng fighters in No 11 Group had to be ismissed. Fighter Command could ot sit back at Stanmore and watch ts forward stations being wiped out. he birds must fight for their own ests and accept the challenge of uperior numbers of enemy fighters. n all, seven Squadrons of Spitfires nd Hurricanes attempted to break p the large Luftwaffe formations but hey were outnumbered and roughly andled by the Me 109s which seemed hat day to be everywhere in the sky.

To the west in the late afternoon it vas another story, some two hundred nd fifty Air Fleet 3 aircraft fanning ut over Hampshire and Wiltshire. he RAF put up more than one undred and thirty fighters from leven Squadrons and so harrassed perrle's Air Fleet that it returned to ase less twenty-five bombers and ighters and without causing much erious damage.

By early evening the battle had wung back to the invasion front of outh-east England, radar plotting nore than seventy 'bandits' winging n from Calais. They were briefed to ttack the vital sector stations at Kenley and Biggin Hill but fortunately

Jnloading: stick of bombs from a Do 17

Before: pilots racing as the alarm rings

After: de-briefing after an action

A Spitfire in its bomb pen
survives a low level strafing run

TARGET ENGLAND
1 Briefed
2 Ready to go
3 Last one on parade
4, 5 & 6 Last minute checks
7 On the way
8 Enemy ahead
9 Target below
10 Bombs away

73

8

9

10

for Park it was the less important field at West Malling that bore the brunt of the attack after his pilots had deflected the raid from its planned targets.

After twenty-four hours the Luftwaffe had completed its numerically largest, and geographically most comprehensive daylight assault of the battle, flying 1,780 sorties, of which more than five hundred were made by bombers. Excepting the astonished units of Air Fleet 5 which had expected an unopposed trip, the German bomber and fighter crews believed they had done well, and claimed the destruction of eighty-two Spitfires and Hurricanes against a true figure of thirty-four. But the Luftwaffe had lost seventy-five aircraft on this single day. Not half as many as the RAF's estimated figure of one hundred and eighty two, but a serious enough blow to prevent any repetition of air attack against Britain on the scale of August 15 – in this battle or, indeed, for all time.

Nightfall on August 15 brought no respite. The Luftwaffe did not expect accurate results from night bombing, although at this stage it was under strict orders from Hitler not to resort to terror bombing of obviously non-military areas. Seventy bombers cruised the length and breadth of Britain primarily to keep air raid sirens wailing, and generally to fatigue a nation which, it was hoped, was beginning to live on its nerves.

Next morning, after the Luftwaffe's unprecedented effort and the RAF's resilient defence on August 15, the operational activities of Air Fleets 2 and 3 were greatly reduced and Air Fleet 5 was virtually out of the battle. Nevertheless the Luftwaffe managed to fly 1,700 sorties – a heavy enough volume to sustain Goering's boast that he would drive the RAF out of the skies of south-east England within a matter of days. Indeed, the Luftwaffe leaders, surprised though they were by the RAF's continuing resistance, believed that Dowding's defeat was imminent. Their sums told them that the RAF had lost 574 fighters in the air since early July and that other losses brought the total to 770 aircraft. Taking its estimated British production figures into account, the Luftwaffe credited the RAF with some three-hundred serviceable aircraft out of a total of 430 fighters.

In truth, new fighters leaving the factories at the rate of one hundred a week amounted to some seven-hundred and fifty Spitfires and Hurricanes since the beginning of July. Two-hundred and thirty-five of these fighters were awaiting immediate issue to join nearly six hundred operational fighters in forty-seven Spitfire and Hurricane Squadrons of Fighter Command.

As the Luftwaffe, on August 16, had but some seven hundred Me 109 fighters in Air Fleets 2 and 3, Dowding was equipped to meet fighter for fighter were he minded to commit his entire force to the invasion front. But, like Park who had been saving for his rainy day in No 11 Group, Dowding with four Groups under his order in Fighter Command had been saving on a broader basis. And even now he was not prepared to spend his savings. So long as all the signs pointed towards invasion Dowding saw it as his duty to provide protection for all areas of Britain against the threat of bombing and at the same time to keep the fighter Squadrons outside the localised battle area in reserve for the very worst that could happen – a landing and a march on London.

Thus, at the most, there were not more than three-hundred Spitfires and Hurricanes in southern England to do battle. The Luftwaffe, believing that Dowding was down to the last dregs of his fighter Squadrons, resumed daylight raids on August 16.

The fabled few

On August 16 airfields were again the primary targets of the Luftwaffe. At midday seventy strongly escorted bombers broke through persistent fighter interference to bomb West Malling. The bombers would have been more usefully employed against a permanent sector station. But, as the RAF now thankfully knew, the Luftwaffe lacked the selectivity that preparation and accurate intelligence would have given them. Westwards, attacks were made on a pair of naval and coastal command airfields, neither of which rated priority at this critical stage of the battle. It was a different story, however, at Tangmere, No 11 Group's most westerly sector station. Here, Park's pilots experienced the nightmare situation of returning to land and refuel while their airfield was being dive-bombed.

Among the pilots trying to put his Spitfire down while the Stukas were overhead was Pilot Officer Billy Fiske, the American who need not have been there. As Fiske flew in, his Spitfire smoking, wheels retracted and jammed, Tangmere was being 'pasted'.

Every hangar, every workshop, all stores, sickquarters, even the Salvation Army hut, a write-off. Fiske and his fellow pilots were greeted by a scene of dreadful devastation as they made their landings. Nose down through the falling bombs Fiske tried to slither a belly landing on the cratered airfield. For a moment it seemed that the American volunteer was safely home, although he still had to survive the raid in progress. Then, horrifyingly, the Spitfire was enveloped by flames. Pilot Officer Fiske died shortly afterwards from his injuries. At St Paul's Cathedral in the heart of the city of London there is a tablet placed in memory of Billy Fiske, 'An American citizen who died that England might live'.

Death and injury by burning was an ever present hazard in the cockpits of the RAF fighters of 1940, especially in the Hurricane Squadrons. A pilot who failed to escape did not survive more than a minute in a blazing Hurricane. On this summer's day of August, 1940, Flight Lieutenant Nicholson, formerly a Spitfire pilot of

No 72 Squadron and now with No 249 Squadron of Hurricanes, was patrolling Southampton in cloudless sky and wondering if the baby which his wife was expecting up north in Yorkshire had arrived. He was hoping, too, for a 'squirt', as fighter pilots said, at the enemy – and then there they were, three Ju 88 bombers, a little way ahead.

Accompanied by two other Hurricane pilots, Flight Lieutenant Nicholson was closing fast on the bombers when to his annoyance he saw that a Squadron of Spitfires had raced him to the prey. The Junkers were disposed of in moments. Disappointed, Nicholson began the long climb to return to the remainder of his patrolling Squadron. But he was not to reach their safer altitude. An Me 110 had slipped unseen onto his tail and was pumping cannon fire into the Hurricane. In seconds, Nicholson's fighter was blazing, the pilot blinded by blood in one eye and wounded in a leg.

In these circumstances the Flight Lieutenant ought to have attempted an escape. But he had as yet to shoot a German down and he was determined to make his attacker his first victim. Throwing the Hurricane to starboard, Nicholson saw the 110 hurtle past and straight into the gunsight. Diving at 400 mph the Hurricane was now a burning hell, but Nicholson kept on the tail of the enemy fighter until he saw it crash into the sea. Only then did he decide it was time to abandon ship. But his thumb on the firing button and his hand on the throttle were seared by flame. Desperately, he fought to free himself from the cockpit seat straps. Even when he had released himself and was somersaulting earthwards, Nicholson faced another test of endurance. But somehow he managed to tear at the ripcord of his parachute with a pair of badly burned hands. Ordinarily, the fighter pilot's ordeal would now have been almost over but two more hazards faced Nicholson before he could be sure that he had jumped to fight another day. Floating over Hampshire at the end of a parachute he was closely inspected by an enemy fighter pilot who, exhibiting good manners, left him to the tender mercies of a Home Guard military

unit on the ground. For as Nicholson came to earth, riflemen of this army of volunteers hastily recruited for the expected invasion, fired at the British pilot. Fortunately, their aim was poor and Flight Lieutenant Nicholson survived to receive the Victoria Cross, the only VC awarded to a fighter pilot in the Battle of Britain.

Hammering away at the airfields, the Luftwaffe was strategically correct if it intended to meet Goering's expectation of air superiority within four clear days. But, throughout the length and breadth of Britain there were different sorts of airfields and before the end of daylight operations on August 16 the Luftwaffe again made a most successful, but in the circumstances, a wholly wasted effort. On this occasion it picked out a bomber training station and maintenance unit at Brize Norton. Forty-six Oxford aircraft were destroyed on the ground – but aircraft which could not possibly influence a pre-invasion bid for air superiority.

However, fresh and more intelligent attacks on the fighter defences in south-east England were being planned. August 17 was a quiet day, but Sunday August 18 1940 gave promise from midday of repeated attacks that would test the RAF to the limit.

In the event the raids were not so heavy as those of the 15th. But what the Luftwaffe lacked in numbers it compensated in determination to reach and to bomb airfields along the bomber path to London.

By now Luftwaffe commanders had grown more respectful of the RAF's radar directed interception and were experimenting with methods of eluding it. On August 18 Park's important sector station at Biggin Hill was singled out for one such ruse, even though the plan was incomplete in its execution.

The ruse was to send in a pair of strong, consecutive high level escorted bomber raids succeeded by a short, sharp, hedge-hopping raid by one squadron of unescorted bombers flying too low to be detected by radar. The death-or-glory boys of this low level wave were to reap the advantage of having their target picked out for them by the fire and smoke caused by the earlier waves of high altitude bombers.

On paper the plan seemed fighter and radar-proof, but in execution it landed the Luftwaffe in a series of rough and unexpected situations which, such was the confusion of the hour, were not wholly of Fighter Command's making.

For the attackers the operation got off to a poor start when the high level Ju 88s were delayed by a rendezvous mix-up over France and the nine Do 17s of the low level attack were obliged to find Biggin Hill without the pathfinding assistance of the Junkers.

Thus it happened that while the two high level formations were lumbering towards Biggin Hill the fast low raiders were almost on top of the target where, to their misfortune, the ground and air defences were standing-by to give them a very hot reception. While Biggin Hill had no inkling of the low level attack – radar had picked up no signal – it was prepared for the expected high level bombers.

But of this the Dornier pilots knew nothing and, to their astonishment, there ahead of them lay the unmistakable sector station of Biggin Hill, tranquil and undisturbed as a service airfield on a peacetime Sunday. There was no time for the Luftwaffe crews to wonder what had gone wrong because suddenly, terrifyingly, they found themselves in a mesh of light and heavy anti-aircraft crossfire from the ground including the new hazard of steel cables projected by rocket and dangling across the airfield from small parachutes. Then, to increase their discomfort, the Dorniers were pounced upon by two of Biggin Hill's three Squadrons which had been waiting for the radar-reported high level formations. Only two of the Dorniers returned safely to France. Eventually the high level raids arrived and, experiencing an equally hot reception, lost four bombers.

Fortunately for Biggin Hill on this occasion, little damage of importance was caused by the raid though the bomb craters, and particularly the unexploded bomb holes caused great inconvenience. When the raid was over a sergeant of the Women's Auxiliary Air Force was seen picking her way round the craters and marking unexploded bombs from the bundle of red

4.7 ack-ack guns in action

'Angels'. RAF slang became an integral part of the English language

'Bandits' over Biggin Hill

flags stuffed under one arm. During the raid twenty-eight year old Sergeant Joan Mortimer had shown conspicuous gallantry in helping to keep ammunition moving to the gun positions and now, still risking her life, she was ensuring that Biggin Hill remained operational. It was later announced that Sergeant Joan had been awarded the Military Medal, a man's medal for a girl's bravery in the face of the enemy.

While Biggin Hill was under attack Kenley, just six miles westward, came in for a 'pasting' in similar circumstances and, sadly for the defenders, less went wrong for the Luftwaffe in this operation.

Here the high level and low level attacks neatly coincided and some one hundred bombs hit Kenley sector station, destroying six Hurricanes and a number of other less significant aircraft. Ten hangars were wrecked and the departing Dorniers, less several of their number, left Kenley a sore, smoking shambles.

Simultaneously, other Air Fleet 2 raiders hit West Malling and Croydon.

In the afternoon Air Fleet 3 maintained the pressure, attacking airfields in Hampshire and West Sussex. By late afternoon Air Fleet 2 had resumed operations, taking another crack at Croydon. By nightfall when the Luftwaffe crews were preparing to keep Britain awake with widespread nuisance appearances and some accurate minelaying in the Thames Estuary and the Bristol Channel, the defenders could look back on a wearing day, reminiscent of August 15. The RAF had, however, taken their toll of the Luftwaffe: seventy-one German bombers and fighters for the loss of twenty - seven British fighters, in which only ten pilots had been killed.

There were few blessings the RAF could count upon in these hot August days of non-stop fighting but there was one and that was the advantage of fighting a defensive battle over its own terrain and coastal waters.

As the figures for August 18 indicate a fair proportion of RAF fighter pilots were baling out to fight again, a blessing for which no man was more thankful than the commander-in-chief him-

Churchill's 'young chicks'

elf. In mid-August, Dowding's losses
ere mounting. Between August 8 and
ugust 18 he lost one hundred and
ighty three fighters in the air and
ome thirty destroyed on the ground.
n the same period ninety-four fighter
ilots were killed or missing and sixty
ounded, many of them badly burned.
eaverbrook was replacing written off
nd damaged machines at more than
ne hundred a week but there was no
at reserve of trained fighter pilots.
owding's worry was that he might
ose the war for Britain before a new
eneration of fighter pilots was ready
or operational flying. Already as night
ell on August 18 he was scraping the
arrel to the extent that new pilots
oining Squadrons were lucky if they
ad put in more than ten hours Hurri-
ane or Spitfire solo flying.

With this problem weighing heavily
n his mind, Dowding, understand-
bly, looked outside Fighter Com-
and for new 'chicks' as Churchill
ffectionately termed his young air-
nen in their 'teens and twenties.
ould he not add to more than fifty
aval fighter pilots already on loan

from the Fleet Air Arm, trained pilots
from the RAF Bomber and Coastal
Commands? Such pilots might not
meet the training requirements of a
peace-time Fighter Command but
they were service-trained men and
wore air force wings. Unhappily, the
fighter chief's requests were received
coolly at Air Ministry. Each command was responsibly conscious of the
demand that might fall upon it if an
invasion fleet put to sea. Just as
Dowding had been saving his fighters
for *his* rainy day, the air staff were
husbanding the remainder of the air
force against the invasion which only
Dowding's denial of Luftwaffe air
superiority could prevent. When
Dowding asked for all the more experienced pilots among the Fairey Battle
crews of Bomber Command the air
staff opposed transfer because they
were holding these obsolescent
machines in readiness for attacks on
landing barges. Eventually, under
great pressure from the fighter chief,
the air staff agreed on a ration of pilots
from outside Fighter Command.
Dowding was loaned twenty Fairey

Sqd Ldr Peter Townsend DFC, with members of his squadron
Left: **Father and daughter**

Battle pilots and thirty-three pilots from Army Co-operation Command Squadrons, fifty-three airmen who, after a course of only six days were un-buttoning their uniform jacket top buttons and fighting and dying with that gallant band of airmen whom Winston Churchill was about to immortalise as the famous 'Few'.

Addressing the House of Commons on the general war situation on August 20, 1940, the Prime Minister said, 'The gratitude of every home in our island, in our empire, and indeed throughout the world, except in the abodes of the guilty, goes out to the British airmen who, undaunted by odds, unwearied in their constant challenge and mortal danger, are turning the tide of the world war by their prowess and by their devotion. *Never in the field of human conflict was so much owed by so many to so few.* All hearts go out to the fighter pilots, whose brilliant actions we see with our own eyes every day . . . '

Brilliantly, intuitively, Winston Churchill had wrought and had spoken with perfect timing the phrase which will be remembered and repeated so long as Britain honours the memory of the four hundred and fifteen pilots who fell in her defence in the Battle of Britain, 1940.

As daylight faded on August 18, the four days which Hermann Goering had estimated as being sufficient to gain air superiority over southern England, had passed into history; and the two weeks' grace which Hitler had allowed himself before reaching a decision on Operation Sea-lion, the invasion of England, were slipping by, Perceptibly, the Battle of Britain was going against the Luftwaffe and within the Air Fleets German acceptance of this truth was reflected with the smallest beginnings of a loss of heart. It was hardly surprising, therefore, that the Luftwaffe fighter ace, Adolf Galland, was telling the Commander-in-Chief to his face that he would prefer a wing of Spitfires to his German Me 109s.

The operational Spitfire of August, 1940, could have received no greater citation. Its performance had im-

Major Adolf Galland. One of the greatest fighter aces of all time
Left: **Goering with senior Luftwaffe officers during the battle**

proved greatly on that with which it had entered the war, an improvement which, as with the birth of the Spitfire, was largely due to personal initiative and private enterprise.

For some while Captain Geoffrey de Havilland, the pioneer aircraft manufacturer who had designed and flown fighters in the first world war, had been convinced that the margin between the fighters' existing variable pitch, and the constant speed propellers the adoption of which he had been strongly urging, might prove mortal to the nation.

Unable to obtain official sanction for a conversion programme, de Havilland had arranged privately with a squadron to convert a single fighter. News of a miraculous improvement in performance spread from squadron to squadron and the authorities found themselves bombarded with requests for conversion.

Risking that his company might

'The Enemy'
1 The lucky mascot
2 The anxious moment
3 Goering's 'young chicks'
4 Safe home
5 The tally
6 Domestic service

4

5

6

never be paid for the work, de Havilland sent teams of engineers from airfield to airfield to convert the front line fighters. The contracts caught up with the work later.

Engine performance had improved too. Among the technical deficiencies of the Spitfire and the Hurricane earlier in the battle was that of carburettor trouble. Luftwaffe fighter pilots had quickly learned that they could evade a fighter on the tail by going into a power dive. The reason for this was that the carburettor of the Merlin engine was flummoxed by the sudden flop from the horizontal to the vertical, obliging RAF pilots to roll on their backs and then to dive. Rolls-Royce quickly devised a float-less carburettor and made the Spitfire even more attractive to Galland and his comrades.

When Galland asked Goering for Spitfires, there was less cynicism in the request than the apparent cheek infers. The manoeuvrable Spitfire would have been more compatible than its superior, the Me 109, with new instructions which the Nazi commander-in-chief now issued.

Alarmed by bomber losses, and the falling morale among bomber crews, Georing insisted that Me 109 pilots must stick close to their charges, a particularly awkward and restricting assignment when accompanying the slow and vulnerable Stuka dive-bombers.

Thus, while the morale of the bomber crews was being undermined by their losses, the offensive spirit of the fighter pilots was about to be sapped by this reining-in of their desire to hunt and destroy the RAF's defending fighters, the principal object of the attack of the eagles. Moreover, the Me 109 pilots were especially irked at being expected to nurse the Luftwaffe's failed long-range fighter, the Me 110.

Just how hazardously short was the Me 109's own range for the trip to London has been emphasised by Galland in his book 'The First and the Last'. 'The short range of the Me 109 became more and more of a disadvantage. During a single sortie of my wing we lost twelve fighter planes, not by enemy action but simply because after two hours flying time

the bombers we were escorting had not yet reached the mainland on their return journey. Five of these fighters managed to make a pancake landing on the French shore with their last drop of fuel, seven of them landing in the 'drink'.''

But Hermann Goering was not minded to give ear to the up-to-the minute experience behind Galland's cynical remark. He still regarded these high summer operations against Britain as the consummation of everything he had ever dreamed of for his Luftwaffe. Like a gambler who feels certain he will win on the next throw, he remained confident that given another four days of fine weather, he could claim victory. Sending Kesselring and Sperrle back to their Air Fleets from a conference, held in his dream world at Karinhall, the Commander-in-Chief ordered the Field Marshals to subject the enemy to the ordeal of bombing round the clock. But bad weather conditions intervened and brought the RAF a much needed rest on August 19. It was not until August 24 that this new phase of the Battle of Britain began in earnest.

The miraculous mistake

If Germany was to invade Britain before the fair campaigning weather of late summer and early autumn gave way to the fogs and storms of an English winter, Hermann Goering's round-the-clock command had been given at the critical moment. The Commander-in-Chief of the Luftwaffe was now as much at war with the clock as with the Royal Air Force. On August 24, the calendar reminded him that only three days remained before Hitler's next declared deadline for a decision – to invade or not to invade.

Goering comforted himself that bad and changeable weather had robbed him of the reduction of Britain's fighter defences in four days. Now the weather had improved over southern England. It was fine and cloudless. Three days of this favourable weather and it would be all over.

In No 11 Group, where they welcomed poor weather, the days of respite had meant operational aircraft preserved, new fighters built and delivered, pilots rested and pilots reprieved. The clear, cloudless dawn of Saturday, August 24, was greeted with great apprehension.

The sector controllers expected the worst and by nine in the morning radar confirmed that the Luftwaffe was massing over Cap Gris-Nez opposite Dover. There was no question today of a Luftwaffe muddle; of fighters failing to rendezvous with bombers. Here they came, one hundred bombers and fighters, stepped-up from 12,000 to 24,000 feet and heading for Dover. But were they coming? Appreciating the effectiveness of the coastal radar chain, and having abandoned hope of destroying its individual sites, the Luftwaffe was now intent upon foxing them. Keeping aircraft in the air opposite Dover, Kesselring had Park guessing. A feint might remain a feint or develop into a mass attack, and as though this was not confusing enough, the RAF's radar was unable to differentiate between fighters and bombers. Consequently, No 11 Group found itself obliged to fly several Squadrons on patrol with the consequent risks of pilot fatigue and fuel shortage at the critical moment of attack.

Indeed, just such an incident occurred in mid-morning when the hapless 264 Squadron of Defiants was

Key to victory. The radar masts

The plotting table

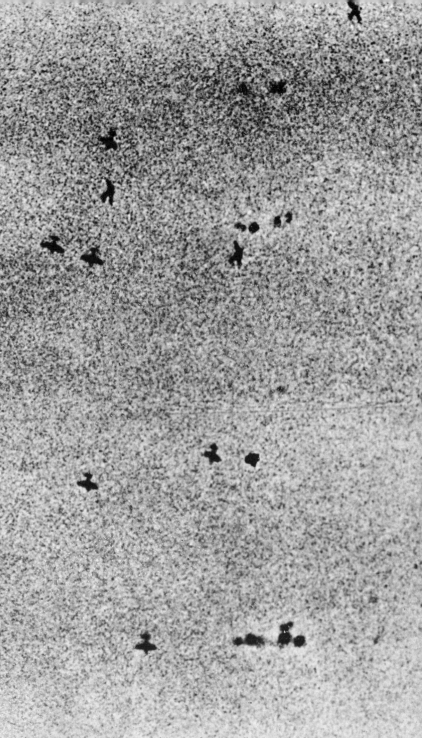

Dog-fight

caught on the ground. Despite the fact that the Defiant had proved to be below standard as a day fighter, No 264 Squadron had been ordered south from Yorkshire to reinforce No 11 Group at Hornchurch. Unsuited to the fast-climbing role of defending a cliff-top front line airfield, No 264's Defiants were ordered to Manston at five am on August 24. At 8.30am they were scrambled for the second time since their arrival on the Kent coast, and sent back to Hornchurch. Hardly had they touched down, than they were returned to Manston, where nine of the Squadron's twelve aircraft apiece landed to refuel, while three kept watch above. And then it happened. Seven of the re-fuelled Defiants were about to take-off when twenty Ju 88 bombers, escorted by a swarm of fighters, swept in from the sea, their bombs falling among the Defiant fighters as they struggled into the air. In the melee above Manston three Defiants were destroyed. So, back to Hornchurch flew the survivors, their arrival coinciding with the Luftwaffe's afternoon resumption, target Hornchurch. Again, the Defiant pilots took off through a curtain of falling bombs, losing their fourth aircraft of the day. Next day seven new Defiants were delivered. They looked good but now their limitations were only too well known to their crews. Moreover, as some of the aircraft lacked self-sealing tanks and their Browning guns were unharmonized, it was obvious that the stress of the battle was beginning to tell in the supply organisation. In fact, such was the Squadron's general unfitness for fighting that three days later, when the crews were scrambled again during a raid, only three aircraft were still service-able. Up went the lumbering, slow-climbing, turret-gunned fighters. It was their last appearance in the south of England during the Battle of Britain. The Squadron was withdrawn to the north. The Defiant had had its day as a day fighter.

As the fighting swayed to and fro across southern England on August 24, with Air Fleet 3 putting in a major daylight appearance over Southampton and Portsmouth in the south-west, the defenders were uncomfortably aware that the Luftwaffe had tight-ened its tactics. The fighter chiefs recognised that the heavy attacks against their front line airfields and the new tight defence Me 109 fighters around the bombers, represented the most serious threat they had yet faced.

Kenley, Croydon, Biggin Hill, West Malling, Hornchurch, Rochford, North Weald, Debden, Hawkinge, Lympne, Manston, these airfields were the inner defence ring around London in August and September 1940. On August 24 it was open to question how long these fighter bases could hold out. After four heavy attacks on this desperate day, Manston was wholly abandoned. The retreat seemed ominous.

Nevertheless, while the leaders of the 'Few' were tormented by the prospect of being driven out of south-east England, with all the national and service morale implications of such a retreat, the morale of the pilots soared. Sergeant RF Hamlyn, a clerk who had joined as a weekend flier three years before the war, fought three separate battles between nine am and four pm on August 24 – 'in office hours' as the Luftwaffe's regular daylight appearances were familiarly dubbed by fighter pilots. The Sergeant bagged a Ju 88 and four Me 109s in the office hours he would ordinarily have spent at a desk. But the 'Few' could not have flown and fought successfully without the hardworking ground crews in greasy overalls who carried out the unglamorous, hazardous job of re-fuelling the fighters under fire, and who worked all hours to keep their pilots in the air. On this desperate Saturday towards the end of August 1940, there took place an exchange of memoranda which bears eloquent witness to the team spirit existing between these ground crews and their pilots.

Returning from a dogfight, a Squadron Commander found a note on his desk. 'From NCOs and men of No 609 Squadron to Squadron Leader Darley and all pilots of No 609 Squadron: In view of the recent successes achieved by the RAF and No 609 Squadron in particular, we wish to offer all pilots our sincerest congratulations and "Good Hunting" for the future. We feel honoured to have such

The end of a DO-17

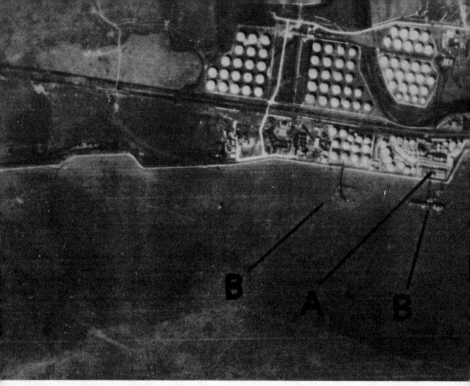

Briefing photograph for Luftwaffe crews. Because some crews missed this target and bombed London, the hard pressed fighter command gained time for recovery. 'One of the greatest miscalculations of history'

excellent pilots in the aircraft we service.'

'Good Hunting!' Discounting the damage on the airfields, it had been a profitable day for Dowding's Spitfire and Hurricane pilots, the Luftwaffe losing thirty-eight fighters and bombers to the RAF's twenty-two fighters.

At this point, as summer slid into early autumn, the aerial duel between the Luftwaffe and the Royal Air Force had been fought almost continuously for six weeks. Yet the British people for the most part were curiously divorced from the perilous reality of their situation.

In the sky over southern England airmen were fighting a desperate battle for the survival of the country. But outside the battle, life continued in its familiar pattern. Cricket, the national summer sport, was still played and scores were reported in the press, albeit as afterthoughts to the daily scores of this new and more exciting contest, RAF v Luftwaffe. It was an ideal of nonchalant nonchalance dear to Britons who rejoiced in its projection to the world. When tennis was replaced by pig farming at Wimbledon, the secretary of the internationally renowned All England Tennis Club explained humorously, 'There is little tennis and we must do something.'

Theatres were thriving in London's west end. At the Piccadilly Theatre Robert Donat was opening in 'The Devil's Disciple', Shaw's satire on the behaviour of the Red Coats in America. In view of the British Army's recent evacuation from Dunkirk, one line in the play was highly topical: 'The British soldier can stand up to anything Sir, except the British War Office'. A vegetarian himself, George Bernard Shaw delighted the nation by observing 'There is nothing wrong with the official meatless and eggless ration which is virtually my own diet. I cannot, however, guarantee that England will become a nation of Bernard Shaws on it. That

B Tham

would be too much to hope for.'

Such humour abounded. Not the strained joking of desperate people but the humour of light comment and asides, conveying the British enchantment with being up against the wall. And then between nightfall on August 24 and dawn on August 25 something happened that was to change all this. London was bombed.

It was a mistake, a mistake of historic proportions, and it was made not because Hitler had ordered terror attacks on historic buildings and non-combatant civilians, but for the simple reason that some of his bomber crews, briefed to attack Thameshaven oil targets east of the old narrow streets of the banking and commercial quarters of London, had lost their way. 'One of the greatest miscalculations of history,' as Hanson Baldwin of the New York Times commented years afterwards, this navigational error by ten of the one hundred and seventy bombers over Britain that night, set off a sequence of events which was to lead to the destruction of so much of Germany, to Dresden and eventually to Hiroshima. More imme-

diately, as will shortly emerge, it was to deflect the Luftwaffe from the bombing plan that might have led to victory in the Battle of Britain. Almost before the nation could draw breath to cry out for retaliation, and indeed before the smoke and the dust had settled on the crumbled church of St. Giles at Cripplegate and other ruins in the heart of the city, a force of more than eighty RAF bombers was winging that night towards Berlin. In fact, the British crews were specifically briefed to attack military objectives or to bring their bombs back; in fact only twenty-one bombers unloaded on Berlin; in fact twenty-one crews brought their bomb loads home. But retaliation called for retaliation, and very soon escalation, as it would be termed nowadays, took place.

To this point bombing by both the Luftwaffe and the RAF had been mutually scrupulous. The Luftwaffe had bombed only those objectives it thought would help to speed air superiority and successful invasion. Obviously civilians died and property was destroyed and damaged because

101

Sinister silhouette. Do 17

Ju 88 with Me 109 escort. Gunsight shadow cast on canopy in front of camera

Nerve centre of a fighter station

of inaccuracy and panic unloading, but until the RAF raid on Berlin the air war was cleaner than air war would ever be again. The Luftwaffe had sought out shipping, naval bases, airfields, aircraft factories, railway targets, oil targets. The RAF had dropped leaflets, attacked invasion ports and industrial targets. Soon, standards on both sides would slip until no further scruple remained against using the bomb and the bomber as weapons of terror.

On the night of August 25-26, as Wellington, Hampden and Whitley heavy bombers of the Bomber Command of the Royal Air Force momentarily stole the thunder from their little sisters, the Spitfire and the Hurricane, Dowding was not to know that anger at the Berlin raid would tick like a time bomb in Hitler's brain; that the eventual explosion would save his front-line sector stations and airfields from the threat of extinction.

At this juncture, as the British people enjoyed the tonic wine of retribution, the British fighter chief was preoccupied by two urgent problems of which the public was largely unaware; the rapidly increasing numbers of Luftwaffe bombers roaming at will over Britain after dark, and the deterioration of fighter defence in the south-eastern invasion corner of England. Radar techniques for night fighting and anti-aircraft gunnery being in their infancy, the Luftwaffe was virtually unchallenged after dark. Ill-equipped to defend against the night raiders, the RAF was comforted only by the fact that the Luftwaffe was equally inept in navigation and in finding their assignment targets in the dark.

For instance, most of the one hundred and fifty Luftwaffe bombers sent off on three successive nights to hit the Liverpool docks went so far astray that the defenders were unable to deduce that the Liverpool docks had been the intended target. Even so, the very presence of night raiders was a considerable worry. Droning, sleep-stealing and maddeningly elusive they disturbed the rest of fatigued factory workers and generally took their toll of the nation's nerves.

For the moment, the defenders could do little more than shrug off the night attacks while hastening research into scientific means of shooting down raiders after dark.

Goering continued to expect that Britain would crack under the impact of his round-the-clock offensive but Germany's campaigning weeks for 1940 were slipping away. August 27 had been set as the day of decision for Operation Sealion, but the day came and once again the Führer hesitated Kesselring's fighter leader, General Kurt von Doering categorically claimed 'unlimited fighter superiority', but Hitler had his doubts. In that suspicious mind Luftwaffe losses, as reported, did not justify von Doering' optimistic opinion. Leave it another ten days, Hitler decided, and the British might yet be ready to talk the peace which would free him of this bogey of invasion. Thus, Hitler left the Luftwaffe to prove the validity of von Doering's claim. And between August 30 and September 6 it very nearly did

On the face of it von Doering's estimate was wildly inaccurate, for hard on his claim of unlimited fighter superiority came a day when Fighter Command flew one thousand sorties. This did not mean that Dowding could deploy one thousand fighters. The defence of the front line airfields rested primarily on some two hundred Hurricanes and Spitfires in Park's No 11 Group, on tired veterans and green newcomers flying several sorties a day, and very often in patched-up aircraft. In these circumstances, the raiders, feinting and foxing radar to an increasing extent and closely guarded by Luftwaffe fighters, were getting through and savaging Park's vital sector stations.

The Luftwaffe, eavesdropping on RAF fighter radio communications from its monitoring station at Wissant, noted carefully the arrival of newcomers and rejoiced when Squadrons from the north of England replaced worn out but experienced Squadrons in the battle. New voices betokened a rise in RAF losses, as unblooded pilots sought to prove themselves in battle.

Sector station and squadron operation record books of the period illuminate the tragedy. RAF Hornchurch August 27, 1940, for example:

'In the afternoon 65 Squadron left us for a period at Turnhouse and 603 Squadron replaced them.' Behind this bare administrative record lay the replacement of a battle-trained Spitfire Squadron by a Squadron of green pre-war weekend fliers. These were some of the legendary long haired boys, sons of wealthy and aristocratic families, fresh from school and university, laughingly boisterous, hard living young men who carried the sport of the hunting shires into the skies over southern England.

When No 603 (City of Edinburgh) Squadron's call came some of the pilots were shooting on their station commander, the Duke of Hamilton's grouse moors.

Not a day passed as August slipped into September when the airfields were not under the most extreme pressure. Two attacks stand out as examples of the ordeal on the fighter stations, attacks which brought to a climax on the last day of August and the first of September 1940, a battle within the Battle of Britain, the battle of Biggin Hill. Regularly the recipient of flattering Luftwaffe attention

Target areas. Liverpool Docks
Above: RAF airfield south of London

105

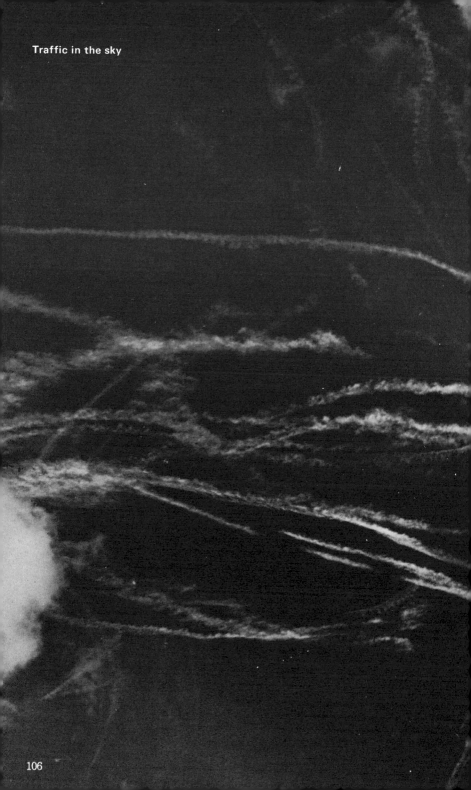

Traffic in the sky

Biggin Hill, Park's sector station in front of London, was expecting more trouble on August 31. A short, sharp low-level attack on the thirtieth had wrecked the airfield and most of its buildings, killing thirty-nine and wounding twenty-six. Ordinarily such loss of life and destruction would have necessitated an operational withdrawal. Yet, miraculously, the survivors got Biggin going again for the next day's business.

Fortunately, the operations block had remained intact. Here, wearing soldiers' tin hats – their 'battle bowlers' they called them – shirt-sleeved girls of the Women's Auxiliary Air Force kept telephone touch with the outside world over lines repaired after each raid, while other WAAFs plotted the approaching raiders. Even when the bombers were immediately overhead the girls remained at their posts, devotion to duty which called for more than ordinary courage after the carnage of the preceding day. As the bombs rained down the whole airfield shook and trembled as though engulfed by an earthquake, and one bomb hit the operations block. But it was not until late in the afternoon of the next day, September 1, that Biggin suffered the worst of its ordeal. After a morning raid, the sixth in three days – the girls in the operations room had yet again plotted the raiders right over their heads and this time the bomb aimers made no mistake. The operations room was demolished. Such was the bravery of two WAAF telephone operators, Sergeant Helen Turner and Corporal Elspeth Henderson that they were later decorated with the Military Medal.

The airfields of south-east England were the battle ground where the Battle of Britain could now be won for the Luftwaffe and lost to the Royal Air Force. Biggin Hill was not alone among the airfields being subjected to their worst hammering of the battle. With the coastal fields of Manston, Hawkinge and Lympne heavily battered and almost out of action, the inland fields took the weight of the new blows.

Daily the German formations built up over France into morning and afternoon waves of two to three hundred bombers and fighters, fanning out over the channel and splitting into tens and twenties, sometimes thirties and forties, as they broke away towards their pre-selected target airfields. Nor was there respite at night.

By September 6 the strain south of London, in the invasion corner of England, was almost intolerable. Operations rooms wrecked, airfields holed with scores of bomb craters, the Fighter Command of the Royal Air Force was reeling. Then, with victory almost in sight, the Luftwaffe stopped short, and hurled itself on London.

Angered by Churchill's reprisal raid on Berlin Hitler stepped in. On September 4, the German leader climbed the rostrum at the Berlin Sportspalast and shrieked invective at Churchill and at Britain:

'I have waited three months without responding, with the thought that they might stop this mischief. Herr Churchill saw in this a sign of weakness. . . . When they declare that they will attack our cities in great strength, then we will eradicate their cities.'

But, as he spoke, there was only one city in Hitler's mind, and fortunately for Britain neither Hermann Goering nor any of his military professionals dared argue with the Führer about the wisdom of his decision.

Indeed, far from even suggesting that Hitler was tactically wrong, Goering and his Luftwaffe leaders convinced themselves that this shift of emphasis was intuitively correct.

Wholly misinformed as to the true state of Britain's daylight fighter defences by over-optimistic intelligence reports, the Luftwaffe believed that the attack on London would drive Dowding into reinforcing his defence with the dregs of Fighter Command reserves from the Midlands and the north – a final harvest for vastly superior numbers of German fighters. As ignorant about the accuracy and effectiveness of night bombing as it was about the RAF fighter strength, the Luftwaffe further believed that heavy unopposed night attacks would destroy London's dockland and essential services. With the approach of winter the Luftwaffe was ready to gamble on yet another short-cut to victory and London looked just right and ripe for the purpose.

London reels

Hermann Goering was convinced that the end of British resistance was in sight. Eager to be with his Luftwaffe pilots in their hour of triumph, the Commander-in-Chief rolled up in his sumptuous personal train at the Pas de Calais. From the cliffs at Cap Gris-Nez late in the afternoon of Saturday, September 7, the Reich Marshal looked across the Straits of Dover at the misty outline of England. He had arrived to cheer on the three hundred bombers and six hundred fighters massing overhead. They were destined for London, twenty two miles across the sea and fifty miles inland from the Kent coast. A short enough trip for a bomber but hazardously far in 1940 for the short-ranged Me 109 fighters which could expect combat anywhere along the outward and return journies.

Up there, leading his wing of Dornier 17s flew that same Colonel Fink who had searched the sky so anxiously for fighters on the fateful morning of August 13 when the muddle over the attack of the eagles had cost him a fighter escort.

Today, perversely, the very presence of swarms of fighters gave rise to almost as much anxiety as had their absence on Eagle Day. Emptying fuel tanks might remove the Me 109 escort at the moments when it was most needed.

But on the first leg of the trip Fink and his crews were lucky again. Late this September afternoon the RAF was hardly in evidence and the bombers were permitted a clear, daylight approach to east London's dockland where they dropped more than three hundred tons of high explosive bombs.

The defenders, misinterpreting the enemy's intentions, let the Luftwaffe through. Following the usual morning attack – this time against Hawkinge – the defenders expected afternoon 'business hours' to bring further raids on sector airfields in conformity with the recent pattern.

By the time the east end of London was ablaze the defenders had recovered their wits and the Luftwaffe's return trip was not to prove so easy. The homing bomber crews were particularly unfortunate to cross the path of No 303 Squadron from Northolt, for this was no ordinary Squadron. Led

Victoria Station. London

Escort patrol Me 109's

by Squadron Leader RG Kellett it comprised highly trained Polish pilots from the peacetime regular Polish Air Force. Escaping from Poland, dispossessed pilots had sworn to avenge the Luftwaffe's devastation of their country. Now, unleashed at last, after months of training to perfect their knowledge of RAF procedures, they whooped with delight as they saw forty Dornier bombers four thousand feet below. Down they went, diving their Spitfires like homing missiles until Kellett and his Polish companions had filled their gunsights with Dorniers. A touch on the gun-buttons, and in a few glorious moments the Poles had destroyed or badly damaged a quarter of the aircraft in the enemy formation, contributing magnificently to the day's final figures. In all, in daylight on Saturday, September 7, the Luftwaffe was engaged by seventeen Squadrons from No 11 Group, one Squadron from No 10 Group, and three from No 12 Group, and lost forty-one bombers to the RAF's twenty-eight fighters. Yet, heavy though its losses were the Luftwaffe was not unduly dismayed. It was the price of quick victory. The war would be over in a few days. Surely with their capital city ablaze and smoking the British would have no heart to continue hostilities. At sunset such was the inferno that it seemed there were two suns in the sky and one of them was setting in the east.

That night the glow simplified German navigation and at nine o'clock the raid on London was renewed by Air Fleet 3. German bomber crews gloated as the capital city of a great empire lay at their mercy, burning and all but un-defended. Other than keeping the bombers at altitude, London's two hundred and sixty four anti-aircraft guns were almost ineffective. Night-fighter defences were non-existent excepting two Blenheim Squadrons and a small night fighter unit experimenting with airborne radar. Thus, undisturbed, two hundred and fifty Air Fleet 3 bombers droned over London. Veterans, cruising above the explosions and great fires in the defenceless city, recalled

They had escaped to fight again.
Polish fighter pilots during the
battle of Britain

the good old days of Guernica, Warsaw and Rotterdam. To heighten the illusion of a joyride, crews turned their radio receivers to BBC dance music and other programmes. English-speaking airmen among the BBCs pirate Luftwaffe listeners must have been bewildered by what they picked-up. In the moment of London's agony, when the German crews believed Britain was on the verge of national disaster, the Luftwaffe listened to Major WH Osman, editor of *The Racing Pigeon* speaking eruditely on the subject of 'Racing Pigeons from the utility angle,' and appealing for support for the pigeon fanciers' Spitfire fund.

However, British quaintness on the BBC was characteristically deceptive. On the German's home front the RAF Berlin raid on the night of August 25-26 had come as a considerable shock to civilians conditioned for a quick end to the war. And now German soldiers, sailors and airmen preparing for Operation Sealion were to learn that the RAF was still capable of making the bombing of airfields and ports a two-way traffic.

On this same Saturday, September 7, as London lay under daylight aerial bombardment, RAF reconnaissance aircraft confirmed that substantial additions were being made to the fleet of invasion barges which had been collecting along the enemy-occupied coast of France and the low countries since the end of August. On the Luftwaffe's airfields, too, changes capable of only one interpretation were taking place. Bombers were flying in from Air Fleet 5 in Scandinavia to reinforce Air Fleet 2 and, more significant, Stuka dive-bombers, hitherto withdrawn from the battle after heavy losses, had reappeared opposite Dover.

Faced with so much photographic evidence and the unprecedented daylight bombing of London, the British chiefs of staff concluded that invasion was imminent. To the British the prospect of enemy landings, the risk of conquest, had never seemed so real since the historic year, 1066, when William the Conqueror from Normandy sailed his knights across the channel and defeated King Harold on a battlefield near Hastings.

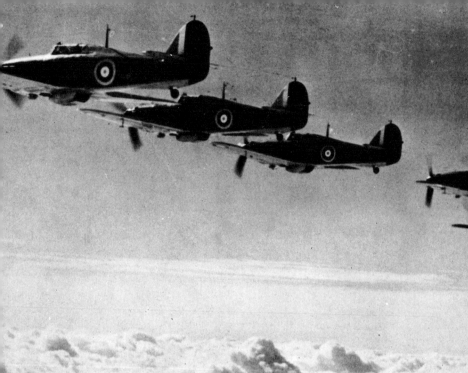

High Summer, 1940: Hurricane patrol

Thus as London crumbled and burned, the British Home Fleet at Scapa Flow prepared to sail south; to fight it out if need be in the narrow confines of the channel. The Army, inadequately equipped after its losses in France, stood-to with the local defence volunteers of the civilian and Home Guard along the shores of southern England.

Invasion imminent! As wave after wave of bombers droned over the coast, and in the direction of London, Army commanders along the beaches could only wonder what the air activity overhead held in store. At any moment they expected their men to be enveloped by a mass descent of paratroops and their ears were cocked for the pre-arranged paratroop alarm, the ringing of church bells in the towns and villages of the invasion areas of coastal England.

And then, over the downs, in the villages, among the seaside holiday towns in some areas, suddenly the wedding bells began to peal. 'This is it' families said as the old, the young and the middle-aged armed themselves with pitch-forks, kitchen knives,

garden tools, indeed with any implements offering a chance of 'taking one with you'.

But it was a false alarm. Neither the Navy, the Army nor indeed the British people as guerilla fighters were called upon to show whether they could have repelled an invading Germany without the Royal Air Force. For Hitler dared not come without the insurance of total air superiority and that was something he was throwing away as he hurled the Luftwaffe against London.

On September 8 German radio stations broadcast the news that Goering had assumed command of Luftwaffe operations against London. For the defenders, the day passed comparatively quietly. Londoners gave thanks for the breathing space and set to work to bury the dead, to dig out the injured, to fight the fires, to get essential services going again, especially at several of the great rail termini which had been badly damaged.

At Fighter Command they thanked God, too. It had only needed an equivalent concentration against Park's bases to rub out No 11 Group. At the same time however, Dowding had to

face up to the disturbing question – what had gone wrong, how had the huge daylight formations got through virtually unopposed? Where, in fact, were the more than three hundred Hurricanes and Spitfires available from Park's twenty-one Squadrons and the immediately neighbouring sectors in Nos 10 and 12 Groups?

Basically the trouble was that the controllers, the men overseeing the plots in the operations rooms, evaluating radar and observer corps reports, had been expecting yesterday's battle. Putting up pairs of Squadrons to cover the sector airfields they had left the goal mouth open.

It had been a costly misinterpretation of the enemy's intention and, as it happened, the error was made in Air Vice-Marshal Park's temporary absence from the operations room at No 11 Group headquarters.

The mistake was not to be repeated next day when late in the afternoon of September 9, nine of Park's Squadrons were up and awaiting a first wave of one hundred heavily escorted bombers and fighters as they approached the coast. Handing off the fighters, Park's pilots assailed the bombers so doggedly that, scattering their bombs, the raiding force wheeled over Kent and Sussex and headed for home.

For the most part the second wave, though harried incessantly and thrown off course, reached the south-western areas of London and scattered its bombs over residential districts far removed from the dockland target areas. On this black Monday for the Luftwaffe, its bomber crews began to wonder whether London would provide the short-cut to victory which they had so confidently expected. It had been an expensive day, twenty-eight aircraft set against the RAF's nineteen fighters on the balance sheet.

If, however, the warm reception of September 9 had taken a little edge off Luftwaffe confidence, it had now become a question of official deliberation in Britain as to how long London could hold out under continuing air attack. In 1940 the sustained bombing of a great capital city was unprecedented and such questions as the breaking

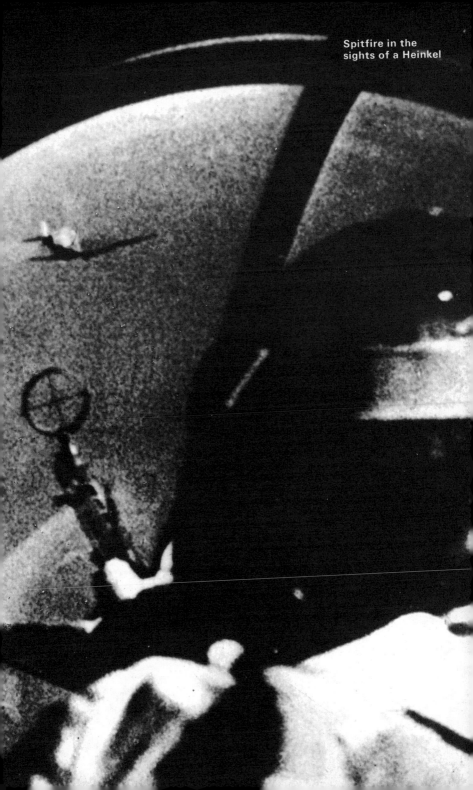

Spitfire in the
sights of a Heinkel

Do 17's over Silvertown, East London.
September 7, 1940

122

point of civilian morale and the ability to restore essential services were unresolved. Coupled with the probability that invasion was imminent – moon and tide were ideal for landings between September 8 and September 10 – the prospect looked exceedingly bleak.

But Hitler remained unpersuaded that sufficient air superiority had been obtained to ensure a successful invasion. On September 10 he announced he would make his decision on September 14, in effect postponing Operation Sealion, if it was to take place at all, until September 24.

The fact was that daily over the coast, and all along the air route to London, the 'Few' of the RAF were saving Britain. While Goering had gained yet another four days' grace in which to finish off Dowding's fighter defences, Luftwaffe chances of victory were diminishing.

Not that the defenders had the smallest inkling of this minimal turn of the tide at the time.

On September 11 Winston Churchill warned the nation: 'If this invasion is going to be tried at all, it does not seem that it can be long delayed . . . Therefore we must regard the next week or so as a very important period in our history. It ranks with the days when the Spanish Armada was approaching the channel, and Drake was finishing his game of bowls; or when Nelson stood between us and Napoleon's Grand Army at Boulogne. We have read all about this in the history books; but what is happening now is on a far greater scale and of far more consequence to the life and future of the world and its civilisation than these brave old days of the past.'

On Sunday, September 15, Churchill had a feeling that this would be a special day in history. He did not know that over the weekend Hitler had faltered yet again about invasion, postponing decision from September 14 to September 17. But something told Churchill on this sunny September morning – 'one of those days of autumn when the countryside is at its loveliest' as Park was to recall – that he should call on Park at No 11 Group headquarters.

Thus, shortly after half past ten and

much to the surprise of the WAAF croupier girls shuffling their counters on the operations plot, the Prime Minister walked into the operations room at Uxbridge and at his side was his wife. The Churchills had called as casually as good friends visit neighbours on a sunny Sunday morning and had strolled into an historic situation.

'I don't know' Park said to the Prime Minister 'whether anything will happen today. At present all is quiet', a statement that within a very few minutes proved, as might be expected, to have been tempting providence too far.

Fascinated by the theatricality of the setting Churchill was absorbed as the WAAF plotters began to mark the enemy's first moves. Radar had warned of large numbers of aircraft assembling over the enemy coast. Quietly, unexcitedly the defence was making its disposition. *Sotto voce*, operations officers spoke closely into the mouth-pieces of their telephones issuing orders which sent the pilots of Park's Squadrons scrambling to their cockpits and anti-aircraft gunners to their action stations.

By half past eleven when the first German aircraft crossed the south coast the Churchills had seen Park put eleven of his twenty-one Squadrons into the air, ten Squadrons in five sets of pairs. In support Spitfires of No 609 Squadron were racing in from No 10 Group. Their specific assignment was to cover the aircraft factory at Weybridge and Windsor Castle, the King's weekend home in the grounds of which Beaverbrook was secretly storing new fighters awaiting delivery to Squadrons. In the rear, behind London, a great wing of sixty fighters from five of Air Vice-Marshal Leigh-Mallory's No 12 Group Squadrons was assembling under the leadership of the legless fighter pilot, Squadron Leader Douglas Bader.

Fighter Command had learned the lessons of September 7 and as Churchill studied every move, the operations controllers put into practice Park's remedial instruction of

London burning behind Tower Bridge. September 7, 1940

125

Strike against London. He 111's take off from airfield in France

The crew watch as the enemy coast passes underneath

Front gunner and bomb aimer watch for Spitfires

September 11. Controllers were to pair like Squadrons, Spitfire with Spitfire, Hurricane with Hurricane. The Spitfire Squadrons were to tackle the enemy fighter screen while the Hurricanes engaged the bombers and their huddle of close-escort fighters.

Radar, the electronic 'crow's nest' of Britain, its key sites spared at the very moment when the attacks were critical, had given warning, and now rising from the airfields, spared also in their last desperate moments as the Luftwaffe turned on London, were the Squadrons which would give Kesselring's one hundred bombers and four hundred fighters from Air Fleet 2 a warm welcome.

The Luftwaffe was in trouble from the moment its first aircraft crossed the east Kent coast, yet stoicly, still absolutely confident that they only had to get through to London to bring a quick end to the war, the bomber crews flew on.

All the way to London the British fighters dived and dived into the thick of the great wedge of bombers, sending Dorniers, Junkers and Heinkel bombers burning, exploding into the green fields below, while here and there a luckless Spitfire or Hurricane spiralled smoking, flaming earthwards.

There was no question of reaching the usual targets of dockland and Thames oil installations. The best the harassed crews could manage was to release their bombs over central London and make for home.

Big Ben, symbolically the official emblem of No 11 Group, had just boomed the twelve notes of noon as the bombs began to fall, one bomb whistling into the garden of Buckingham Palace, where it failed to explode.

In their homes, in the streets, in the pubs over a noontime pint of beer Londoners, wondering if this was the prelude to invasion – read in the Sunday newspapers: 'If and when invasion comes, there will be no secrecy. The news will be given by the BBC and the newspapers'. An hour later the BBC's one o'clock news bulletin announced 'The first air raid on the London area today began just over an hour ago'. A minute or two after the sirens had gone, agency messages reported that there was violent anti-aircraft fire in the south-east and that it was being taken up by guns in other parts of the capital. Screaming bombs were heard to fall . . . at least fifty aircraft are said to have been engaged in a battle area over the outskirts of the city.'

The BBC's calm reaction was reassuring. Twenty thousand feet above Broadcasting House RAF fighter pilots were operating. Among them was Squadron Leader John Sample of No 504 Squadron, an estate agent who had learned to fly on weekends before the war. 'Each of us selected his own target' he recalled afterwards. 'Our first attack broke them up pretty nicely. The Dornier I attacked with a burst lasting several seconds began to turn to the left away from his friends. I gave him five seconds and he went away with white smoke streaming behind him'.

'As I broke away and started to make a steep climbing turn I looked over the side. I recognised the river immediately below me through a hole in the clouds. I saw the bends in the river and idly wondered where I was. I didn't recognise it immediately, and then I saw Kennington Oval and I thought to myself, 'That is where they play cricket'. It's queer how in the middle of a battle one can see something on the ground and think of something entirely different from the immediate job in hand . . .

'I found myself very soon below another Dornier which had white smoke coming from it. It was being attacked by Hurricanes and a Spitfire. . . . As I could not see anything else to attack at that moment I went to join in. Coming in to attack I noticed what appeared to be a red light shining in the rear gunner's cockpit, but when I got closer I realised I was looking right through the gunner's cockpit into the pilot and observer's cockpit beyond. The red light was fire.

'I gave it a quick burst and as I passed him on the right I looked in through the big glass nose of the Dornier. It was like a furnace inside. He began to go down and we watched. In a few seconds the tail came off and the bomber did a forward somersault and then went into a spin. After he had done two turns in his spin his wings broke off outboard of the engines, so that all that was left as the blazing aircraft fell was half a fuselage and the wing roots with the engines on the end of them. This dived straight down, just past the edge of a cloud and then the cloud got in the way and I could see no more of him'.

'The battle was over by then. I couldn't see anything else to shoot at so I flew home.'

After re-fuelling and re-arming Squadron Leader Sample's Squadron was scrambled an hour later to meet a new wave of bombers and fighters.

Meanwhile Douglas Bader and his wing of sixty fighters, tearing southwards from behind London confronted the Luftwaffe with the biggest shock it had yet experienced. Spoiling for battle, Bader's wing – part of Leigh-Mallory's aggressive No 12 Group – was crewed by a cosmopolitan collection of pilots widely representative of the allied cause. Flying alongside the two RAF Squadrons were a Squadron of Canadians, a Squadron of Czechs and a Squadron of Poles. Sweeping all before them the furious sixty drove the Luftwaffe into headlong retreat from London to the coast, Hurricanes taking the bombers, Spitfires the fighters.

Below in the streets of London as the last of the enemy departed the air raid sirens sounded the long, relief-bringing note of the 'all clear'. As the fire engines, ambulances and rescue workers struggled in the debris, office staffs came up from cellars and basements to take their interrupted lunch hour.

Many refreshed themselves in the public houses, exchanging bomb stories, tales of narrow excapes, glimpses of the action. In one pub there was an especial attraction. Somebody had brought in a German airman's boot, a knee-high black leather boot, lined with fleece and zippers on both sides, together with, as the gathering gladly observed, a bullet hole. The previous owner died bombing London.

After a terrible mauling on this fateful Sunday morning the Luftwaffe returned in the afternoon and again the defenders were ready. As the fresh wave of one hundred bombers and three hundred fighters crossed the channel, more than two hundred RAF

**Sqd Ldr Douglas Bader, DSO.
The famous legless fighter ace**

fighters climbed in paired Squadrons to their stations before London.

The British fighter pilots' elation at finding themselves in larger formations after anxious, frustrating weeks of flying in threes and sixes – at best nines or twelves – compensated in part for the great fatigue of repeated sorties. It was reassuring, also, to realize that to be shot down was not necessarily to be out of the battle. It was not unknown for a pilot to bale out over London, take a taxi back to his airfield, and be back in the air in a replacement Spitfire or Hurricane that same afternoon. Thanks to Beaverbrook's repair and production organisation, had the RAF lost two hundred fighters on September 15, all but eighteen could have been replaced from that week's output. The scarcity of trained fighter pilots was now more of a problem than the supply of aircraft for them to fly, and Dowding dropped his policy of alternating tired units with Squadrons from outside the invasion area. Temporarily he rein-

Target area below. He 111

rced Park's embattled Squadrons ith the pick of his 'chicks' from the uiet areas.

It was, perhaps, as well. Green pilots id not last long enough to become red veterans, especially as the pitfires could not always prevent the ghter screen of Me 109s from bouncing he slower more vulnerable urricanes.

Notwithstanding such hazards, ark's paired Squadrons harried the uftwaffe's afternoon wave on its way ɔ London as persistently as they had ngaged the morning raiders; but the ombers, accepting their losses, ressed on courageously. Bombs were ropped at random on London through loud and in the blind man's buff of nloading high explosive on a vast prawling capital city some of the ombs damaged railway and other ssential services.

This afternoon, after the bombers' iiserable morning experience at the ands of Bader's fighter wing, esselring's fighter pilots were look-ng for trouble. Erroneous estimates f Luftwaffe victories assured them hat more than two thousand RAF ghters had been destroyed since the tart of the battle, and so they regar-ed the morning's battle as the death hroes of a spent out fighter force sent p desperately to protect London. For his reason they welcomed the appear-nce of RAF Spitfires and Hurricanes n unaccustomedly formidable num-ers. Here, in the skies over London, as the Lutfwaffe's opportunity to natch the air superiority they had een seeking all summer. But the uftwaffe failed. Even the celebrated ghter leader Major Adolf Galland, hortly to visit Berlin for a pat-on-the-ack from Hitler and decoration with)ak Leaves of the Knight's Cross after is fortieth 'kill', drew a blank.

In Britain the scores, as they were ptimistically calculated at the time, lemonstrated a handsome victory for he RAF. Next day when Winston Churchill walked into his Maproom he ead, chalked on the air battle score-ɔoard – Destroyed one hundred and ighty-three, Probables forty-two,)amaged Seventy-five, Lost twenty-ight. The Prime Minister im-mediately congratulated the Royal Air Force, 'Yesterday eclipses all previous records of the Fighter Com-mand. Aided by Squadrons of their Czech and Polish comrades, using only a small proportion of their total strength, and under cloud conditions of some difficulty, they cut to rags and tatters three separate waves of mur-derous assault upon the civil popula-tion of their native land inflicting a certain loss of one hundred and twenty-five bombers and fifty-three fighters upon the enemy, to say nothing of the probables and damaged, while themselves sustaining a loss of twelve pilots and twenty-five machines. These results exceed all expectations and give just and sober confidence in the approaching struggle.'

The figures on the scoreboard and in the Prime Minister's message were inflated as was discovered after the war. Luftwaffe losses at about sixty to the RAF's twenty-six were neverthe-less high enough to end German hopes of a negotiated peace or any certainty of a successful invasion.

That Sunday night the Luftwaffe returned again as one hundred and eighty bombers struck at central London.

Next morning, Hermann Goering's luxury train rolled into Boulogne and the Luftwaffe commander gave his Field Marshals and Generals a lecture. Bad weather, he said, had given the British time to reorganise. Still mesmerised by his prediction, the Commander-in-Chief urged that even now four days of good weather would bring the Luftwaffe the air superiority which had so long eluded it. From the euphoric, sycophantic little world of his special train, the Reich Marshal ordered further large scale attacks, using as many as four hundred bombers at a throw, but only in the best weather. In poor weather Goering said, the enemy was to be denied rest and recovery by repeated appearances of heavily escorted nuisance raiders. In really bad weather single aircraft were to dash in and alarm the defence system.

In Berlin Hitler was taking a more realistic view. He accepted that weather conditions would deteriorate as winter approached and postponed operation Sealion until further

133

notice. Which, in effect, was for ever.

After the war, Sunday, September 15 was recognised as the climactic point of the Battle of Britain and it is the day upon which the nation annually gives thanks for its delivery from invasion and German servitude. In 1940, however, neither the Luftwaffe nor the RAF could tell what the morrow would bring. Invasion remained a very real threat so far as the defenders knew and daylight operations on the scale of September 15 might continue and even intensify. Indeed, had Kesselring and Sperrle had sufficient planes to carry out Goering's latest orders to the letter, Fighter Command would have been hard pressed to stay the course until winter lowered a safety curtain over the channel and south-east England. On September 15 as Churchill was leaving the Uxbridge operations room Park said, 'We are very glad, sir, you have seen this . . . This shows you the limitation of our present resources. They have been strained far beyond their limits today.'

On September 16 poor weather conditions together with the Luftwaffe's hangover from exhaustion after its effort of the preceding twenty-four hours brought the RAF a needed respite. Sunday had been a sparkling summer's day – Monday dawned rainy and overcast with cloud down to three hundred feet. The mercurial quality of British weather was the secret ally which had previously helped to frustrate Goering's 'four day' plans, and now it was to do so again. Had the Luftwaffe commander-in-chief paid more respect to meteorological considerations from the outset it is doubtful whether he would have embarked on his series of four day 'victories'. As it was, when finally the Luftwaffe had grown wise to the British weather, it so confused itself with an amalgam of 'met' reports that Goering had to intervene. Where forecasts conflicted he ordered, decision must lie with the men on the spot, the meteorological expert of the unit undertaking an air operation.

Thankful for low cloud on September 16 Air Vice Marshal Park reconsidered his position in the light of Sunday's fighting. The pairing of like Squadrons after the enemy break through of September 7 – the setting of Hurricanes onto bombers, Spitfires to fighters – had brought an improvement in interception yet Park was by no means satisfied. In practice rendezvous errors and the sporting inclination of fighter pilots to dogfight were preventing the No 11 Group Commander's theory from being fully effective. However, so long as the Luftwaffe squandered its daylight effort on the fruitless target of London, Fighter Command could breathe fairly freely. But supposing the enemy turned back on Biggin Hill, on Kenley on Hornchurch and any of Park's airfields? Supposing a simultaneous assault was made on the aircraft factories? Then the present situation, serious as it was, might deteriorate overnight.

Fortunately for the defenders as September slipped away and the air battle swayed across south-east England, London remained the principal target for day and night raiders. In weight the attacks were much reduced by comparison with those of the Luftwaffe's heyday in late August and early September, but in effect German bombs were opening up great wounds in London the last of which are only now disappearing.

By September 23 after London had suffered some three weeks of continuous raiding, further retaliation on Berlin was ordered. The war cabinet wanted the RAF to mount a terror raid using parachute mines but the Royal Air Force insisted attempts should be made to hit military objectives. Useful targets were difficult enough to hit in any event and the RAF was not prepared to deprive the Luftwaffe of its pride of place as a bomb waster. That night while more than two hundred and sixty German raiders bombed London indiscriminately one hundred and nineteen RAF Wellington, Whitley and Hampden aircraft were ordered to bomb military targets in Berlin. By contrast the British effort was small but the knowledge of retaliation brought a disproportionate sense of comfort and satisfaction to Londoners who were 'taking it' on the same night.

Next morning the Luftwaffe made two early lunges at London. In the afternoon a raid of much greater significance took place. Bombing up wo formations of some twenty Me 09s apiece – that is converting its rize fighter into a fighter-bomber – he Luftwaffe surprised the defenders nd raced through unchallenged to he Spitfire factory at Southampton, he historic birthplace of Mitchell's nother of all the Spitfires the S6B. uckily the factory escaped serious amage but one hundred members of he Supermarine staff died when an ir-raid shelter received a direct hit.

As Dowding had long feared the uftwaffe had picked out a key fighter actory and in pattern with the nemy's passion for short-lived tacti- al crazes could be expected to repeat he operation at Southampton or lsewhere in the next few days.

Next morning, September 25, a force f over fifty escorted bombers dam- ged the Bristol Aeroplane Company's actory badly and caused more than wo hundred and fifty casualties.

These attacks on aircraft factories oupled with the introduction of fast, ard-to-catch fighter bombers, ren- ered it disturbingly evident to the efenders that for all the continuous, f numerically reduced raiding of ondon, the Luftwaffe was recovering he professionalism of its late August ssault on the sector airfields.

As if in confirmation of Fighter ommand's fear a mixed force of more han seventy Me 109s, He 111s and Ju 8s swept up the Solent from their bases n Brittany and treated the Spitfire works at Southampton to an early and npleasant example of pattern bomb- ng. Within minutes seventy tons of ombs had fallen, to such effect that production was halted and three new ighters were destroyed in the shops, giving the Luftwaffe a net gain on the he day. In the air fighting the score had finished at three all.

Again the initiative seemed to have swung back to the Luftwaffe, a swing that was becoming an established fact of life in the Battle of Britain every time the German air force concen- trated, however temporarily, on worthwhile tactical or strategic tar- gets. At the same time the Luftwaffe was bewildering interceptor Squad- rons with a new ruse – interlarding genuine fighter formations with fighter-bombers. Sweeping formations of Me 109s despatched to entice Spit-

fires and Hurricanes into combat could be disregarded with fair immun- ity but sweeps which contained bombers or fighter-bombers demanded attention. It required only a few such bomber strikes on the aircraft fac- tories – dispersal was taking place but was not yet fully effective – to bring air superiority within reach before the arrival of winter.

Fortunately for the defenders most of the high flying fighter sweeps were innocent, excepting their desire to shoot down RAF fighters in unequal combat. On September 27, reverting to the earlier formations – escorted Dornier, Heinkel and Junkers bombers – the Luftwaffe re-discovered its daylight vulnerability. Out of eighty aircraft bound for Bristol and three hundred for London, fifty-five German aircraft were lost to the RAF's twenty-eight.

The role of Dornier, Heinkel and Junkers bombers was almost over. On the last day of September 1940, the Do 17 and He 111 bombers, so effective in Spain, so fruitful in France, joined the Ju 87 Stuka dive-bomber among the aircraft proven obsolete for com- bat over England. The faster, later, Ju 88 fared no better. It was a sad, bad day for the Luftwaffe; forty-seven aircraft – mostly bombers – shot down at a price of twenty RAF fighters.

In under two months the legend of the Luftwaffe's invincibility had been shattered. Bombers which were to have paved the way to victory in just four days, were forced to hide in the night, and the Me 110 long-range fighter was so discredited that it required its own escort of Me 109s as a hit-and-run bomber.

Point of balance

It was now October and in nearly twelve weeks the Luftwaffe had tried every means of using air power to enforce a quick peace with or without conquest. First there had been the parade of strength over the channel. Then, the short, sharp raids on the radar stations, so rightly undertaken, so foolishly abandoned. Next, after wasted attacks on irrelevant targets, the emphasis was shifted to the fighter airfields particularly Park's sector stations. Then, the ordeal of London. Finally, the belated pinpoint bombing of aircraft factories.

Abandoning each new tactic at the moment when it was on the point of succeeding, the Luftwaffe had gained little, lost twenty-five per cent of its operational strength and devalued its reputation.

Viewed from Dowding's command and Park's group headquarters however, the Luftwaffe's performance still caused grave concern. In early October there was still prospect of enough fair weather to make invasion a continuing possibility and the new fighter-bomber tactics were presenting their own problems.

Unhampered by the presence of medium twin-engine bombers the daylight fighter formations swept in at heights of twenty to twenty-five thousand feet evading radar detection and too high for accurate plotting by the Observer Corps. Efforts to report incoming formations by high flying scout aircraft were unsatisfactory and several of the scouts were quickly shot down. The Me 109s performance above twenty-five thousand feet – by virtue of its two-stage supercharger – was even better than that of the emerging Mark 2 Spitfires and Hurricanes.

At night, Fighter Command technique had advanced little during the summer months. October saw six Blenheim and two Defiant night fighter Squadrons in operational service, but their sorties were hit and miss affairs. The night fighter equipped with reliable interception radar still lay in the future, although a handful

London burns beneath the Luftwaffe attack

At night a dreadful beauty clothed the city

of the new radar Beaufighters were on trial. As for the anti-aircraft defences, the searchlights and guns gave more comfort to civilians than trouble to the enemy, and their bark was very much worse than their bite. But the bark was important because the Battle of Britain was now being fought almost as much in the streets of London as in the skies above where the weaving, feathery contrails gave evidence of the great altitude to which the fighters and fighter-bombers had raised the conflict.

Although Sunday, September 15 – Battle of Britain day – marked the culmination of a week of mass raids against the capital, London's subsequent ordeal was in some respects more arduous.

The phrase 'London can take it' was already a cliché in early October but how many more weeks of death and destruction could London really take? Not least among those asking themselves this question was Hermann Goering who hoped now for a breakdown of morale in a terrorised, burning London as a more likely road to victory than the arbitrary 'four days' with which he had mesmerised himself all summer.

Finding it convenient to overlook the original purpose of the mass attacks between September 7 and September 15 – the destruction of the remnants of the RAF which would rise up and give their all in the defence of the capital – the Reich Marshal now demanded the demoralization of the British people through the razing of London.

If sleepless nights, the destruction of familiar streets and landmarks, death and fire, and row upon row of small homes blasted into rubble could combine to demoralize London then the Luftwaffe must surely win the Battle of Britain. Goering had now convinced himself it would end in mid-October; he re-assured his flagging crews, 'Your indefatigable, courageous attacks on the heart of the British Empire, the city of London . . . have reduced British plutocracy to fear and terror. The losses which you have inflicted on the much-vaunted Royal Air Force in determined fighter engagements are irreplaceable.'

But the British will to fight on, nourished by timely exaltation from Churchill, and the fighters rolling off Beaverbrook's production lines made a mockery of the Luftwaffe Commander-in-Chief's claims. The royal family came out of its castles, too, and was suddenly closer to the people in the shared anxieties of all classes. The King and Queen, King George VI and Elizabeth, the parents of Queen Elizabeth, spent many hours in the bombed streets, encouraging firemen, ambulance teams and air-raid workers and sympathising with the bombed-out. It helped, in a way, that Hitler had bombed the King's London home too.

The King, seeking a means of expressing his admiration for the fortitude of civilians and service people – all now equally under fire – introduced two personal decorations for valour inspired by the air raids. Broadcasting from Buckingham Palace, King George VI announced the George Cross and the George Medal and aptly the air-raid sirens could be heard wailing in the background as the King spoke. The George Cross, the King said, would rank second only to the Victoria Cross.

Unexploded bombs and mines already recognised as a menace to airfields and factories, were now closing streets and endangering people in their homes – as the King was only too aware having received one in his own back garden at Buckingham Palace. Among the first recipients of the decorations were the courageous experts of the new Bomb Disposal Units, men such as Lieutenant R Davies of the Royal Engineers who disarmed a high explosive bomb which had landed just outside St Paul's Cathedral.

As October wore on and Londoners settled down to their 'lot' the daylight raiders became progressively more elusive as the fighters and fighter-bombers appeared at ever increasing altitudes.

At twenty to twenty-five thousand feet Park's pilots found the Me 109 and Me 110 raiders remote enough but soon they were operating at thirty thousand feet – a combat altitude which Spitfires and Hurricanes were hard put to reach in time for interception.

The tracking problems of late September and early October

Summer, 1940. London by day.

London by night

For thousands, the best
hope of protection

worsened with the onset of late autumnal weather, and the earliest radar and observer corps warnings sector stations could expect reached them when the raiders were but twenty minutes flying time from London.

Consequently, Air Vice Marshal Park had to reconsider his tactics yet again. It took his pilots up to thirty minutes to reach thirty thousand feet – a factor that, together with the short notice of the enemy's approach, obliged him to fly readiness patrols. 'Bitter experience' Park reminded his operations controllers 'has proved time and again that it is better to intercept the enemy with one Squadron above him than by a whole wing crawling up below, probably after the enemy has dropped his bombs.'

Park's words were penned with feeling for as he wrote high flying raids were coming in regularly. On October 15, a typical day, thirty Messerschmitts bombed London at nine o'clock in the morning, hitting Waterloo Station. Three quarters of an hour later, fifty more Messerschmitts racing in bombed the financial quarters of the city. At half past eleven yet another formation swept across the Thames estuary, and that night there was moonlight raiding all night long. Train service was brought to a standstill at London's five great terminals. The Underground railway was cut at five points, nine hundred fires started, more than four hundred people killed. Luftwaffe losses in the day and night operations totalled fourteen aircraft; the RAF lost fifteen.

Towards the end of October it began to look at Fighter Command as though there would be no end to the nightmare. For there was little that could be done to stop the night raiders and Dowding and Park were still searching for an answer.

After a long summer of incessant fighting the Luftwaffe's new tactics placed an almost intolerable strain on Fighter Command. In August and in the first half of September the fighter Squadrons had at least managed to rest and remain on their airfields between scrambles. Now, however, the need to maintain strong patrols and to fight at thirty thousand feet or even higher was even more exacting physic-

ally on weary pilots who were spending as many as five hours operational flying each day. A fighter pilot's life expectancy in the Battle of Britain has since been assessed at eighty-seven flying hours – or little over a fortnight at the maximum rate of employment. By October 31 four hundred and fifteen out of some fifteen hundred pilots who fought in the Battle had been killed.

When it was all over, when the air Battle of Britain could be viewed in the broader perspective of subsequent global operations, when dates were needed for the history books, British officialdom settled on the period July 10 to October 31 as that of the Battle of Britain. Obviously, air battles were fought before and after the July and October milestones, but history and the inevitable issue of a campaign decoration for aircrew demanded dates. In November, though the nation's position remained perilous, the people seemed to sense that the moment of mortal danger had passed.

Confidence, bordering on complacency returned. Steeplechasing was in full cry and greyhound racing was drawing larger crowds than any other sport. On the golf courses, where Beaverbrook had previously ordered that wrecks of crashed German bombers should remain to impress players with the eccentric and inappropriate nature of their pastime, fairways were now cleared. A current advertisement showed four Spitfires in a blue sky – no Luftwaffe fighters within miles – and read, 'These are the men who when on leave pursue a golf ball with as much determination as they pursue their quarry.'

The British were conditioning themselves to war, even contracting that ugly word blitzkrieg to 'blitz', and managing to make a word of terror sound warm on the lips of the bombed-out, the shelterers and the air raid workers. 'Don't worry' people said 'We'll have a cup of tea when the blitz is over.' Hitler raged that there was worse to come, but the people were reassured. They had met the threat and survived.

By November air raids were accepted among civilians as part of everyday life. Many felt a touch of pride at finding themselves more in the front line than the soldiers. The RAF however,

And at night they came back

147

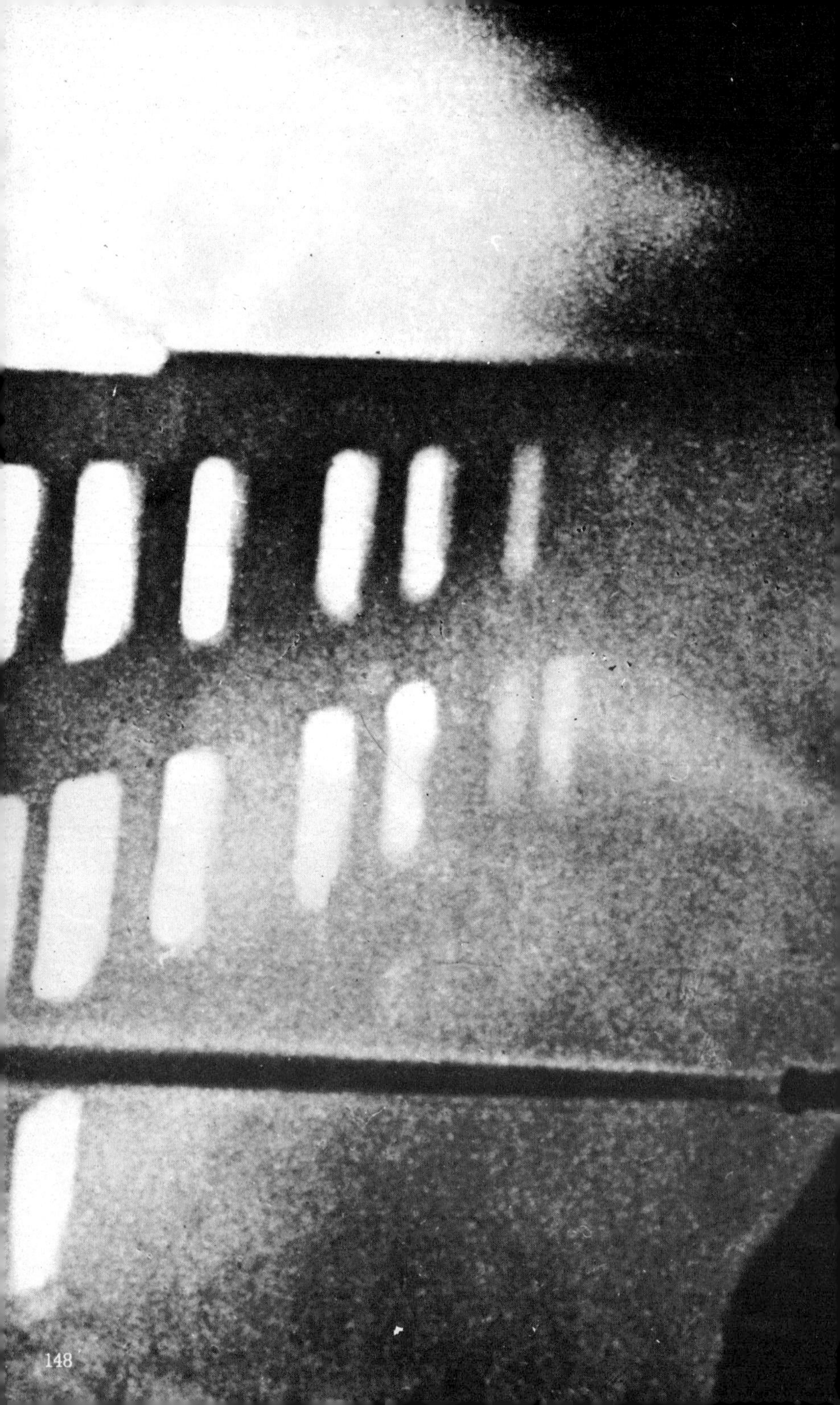

149

So the flames were put out,

the debris cleared away,

could not accept air raids with an equal resignation. It was, after all, their job to keep the enemy out, or at least to deflect him from important targets, and they were not always doing it. Between September 7 and November 13, London was bombed by an average of one hundred and sixty aircraft on 67 consecutive nights, excepting one. With daylight raids tailing off and robbing the RAF of its opportunities to score, dismay over its comparative helplessness at night increased. But there was one moment of comic relief.

To the Luftwaffe's embarrassment, the Italian Air Force, intent upon offering its services as part of Mussolini's contribution to the conquest of Britain, had recently established itself at bases in Belgium. Since late October, Italian bombers had raided harbours along the east coast of England by night. On November 11, introducing a moment of light opera to the fading daylight scene, the Italians, wearing tin hats and bayonets, came by day, meandering over the north sea in ten Fiat BR20 bombers, escorted by forty Fiat CR42 biplane fighters.

After recovering from their astonishment, pilots of two intercepting Hurricane Squadrons, shot down three bombers and three fighters without loss to themselves.

Thus, on a note of light relief, ended the period of major daylight operations against Britain in 1940. On November 14 the bombing of Coventry would usher in a winter of terror bombing up and down Britain. But London could take it, so could the great provincial cities, and the razing of one city centre after another, far from producing a public outcry for peace, confirmed the people in their determination to see the war through. But the story of Britain's winter of terror, of the night blitz which tore the heart out of her cities until Germany's invasion of Russia in 1941 is beyond the scope of this book.

By mid-November the daylight Battle of Britain, which reached its climax on September 15 and continued through the end of October, had fizzled out with the dismal performance of the Italian Air Force. Germany's chance of conquest in 1940 had gone.

and in the morning, London went back to work

153

Verdict of history

What went wrong?

Basically, the Luftwaffe was inappropriately equipped for the Battle of Britain. Earlier success in Spain, Poland, France and Belgium had inspired the German Air Force with an ill-judged idea of its capabilities. In the first place the Luftwaffe's creators, nourishing their brain child on the small print of the Versailles treaty, had built an air arm to support tanks and infantry in the field, a role the Luftwaffe managed magnificently on the continent.

When France fell she fell so rapidly that the Luftwaffe functioned in copybook fashion. In May, 1940, the Luftwaffe's tactical excellence in close support of an advancing army had placed Kesselring and Sperrle's Air Fleets 2 and 3 on the channel coast. Then it seemed to the Air Fleet Commanders that all Britain lay at their mercy. The Air Fleet crews mistakenly saw the channel as a wider, more turbulent Meuse. Only twenty two miles at its narrowest point, it was but one more river to cross, and once across the Luftwaffe would continue its cherished function in tactical support of the army – marching at last on London. It transpired, however, that the Luftwaffe was wrongly equipped to create the prerequisite of invasion, total air superiority over the south-eastern invasion corner of England. Curiously, the disability was accidental.

Leaving aside momentarily the errors of judgment, the mercurial shifts of emphasis that preceded and followed the attack of the eagles in mid-August, 1940, the Luftwaffe lacked one essential weapon for success: the four-engine heavy bomber. Such aircraft would have been available in large numbers but for the accidental death of General Walther Wever, the Luftwaffe's first Chief of Air Staff and Germany's most influential protagonist of the strategic bomber. Far seeing and with a technological turn of mind, Wever planned the mass production of four-engined bombers with a range reaching the north of Scotland, where the British Home Fleet lay in 1940. Under Wever's encouragement the Dornier and Junkers companies in 1936 built prototypes of the Do 19 and Ju 89. But Wever was killed that year an air crash and the Dornier and Junkers strategic bombers which might have won the war for Germany in 1940 died with him. Both aircraft were cancelled by Kesselring in favour of the Stuka dive-bomber and the medium twin-engine bombers which were shortly to become so familiar.

Had Goering possessed a strategic bomber fleet to launch against the radar chain, the sector airfields of No 11 Group, the aircraft factories and perhaps, too, the Royal Navy, his 'four day' dream might have come true. He would still have had to control his shifts of emphasis. But the serious damage caused by medium bombers and fighter-bombers when they attacked worthwhile targets – as in the raid on the Spitfire works at Southampton – shows how decisive a part the cancelled Do 19 and Ju 89 aircraft might have played.

However, Wever died and the Luftwaffe more than justified Kesselring's decision – until it reached the channel coast. Even then it might have created, at worst, fifty-fifty conditions for an invasion but for Goering's chronic inability to find a policy and stick to it. For much of the campaign he was an absentee commander-in-chief, issuing orders from Berlin or Karinhall. A World War I fighter pilot with a fondness for operatic uniforms, Goering was technologically, strategically, tactically ignorant. He remained mentally in the open cockpit, seat-of-the-pants aviation of 1914-1918. He had little concept of the real requirements of modern aerial warfare and it did not help that Hitler knew even less. Had Goering really known his job, had he accepted technological advice, he must for example have appreciated the significance of radar in Dowding's defence system. Luftwaffe intelligence was poor and inaccurate before and throughout the air battle but radar had been no secret since the tall masts had first started to appear before the outbreak of war. The Luftwaffe lost vital ground when it dropped the investigations initiated by the Graf Zeppelin after disappointing results.

Had four-engine bombers saturated the radar sites and rendered the sector stations untenable, then the Stukas could have come back into their own in support of an invading, advancing army. The costly September raids on London, which finally lost the Luftwaffe any chance of winning air superiority over Britain, would not have taken place.

In sum, then, a flying corps d'elite – until September casualties changed this – of some very fine men, let down by some very poor leadership, gave of its best in some excellent but miscast flying machines. Of such men Dowding, the supreme architect of their defeat said, 'They were worthy foes and they went on. They had a terrific gruelling and they stuck it for a long time.'

Could Britain have done better?

Superficially, the question appears impertinent. National survival was at stake and the RAF assured it. It fought against overwhelming odds at the start of the battle and stayed the course to take advantage of the enemy's mistakes and its own experience. Of paramount importance, it stripped the German air force of self-confidence and an outsize reputation for invincibility.

In London and the great provincial cities of Britain civilians supported 'The few' by demonstrating a magnificent morale under fire. While the defeat of the Luftwaffe in the air incurred an un-repayable debt to 'The Few', the stoicism of civilians carrying on under the inspiration of Winston Churchill incurred an almost equal debt. In twelve weeks the nation was preserved by a spiritual partnership stimulated by Churchill and existing between pilot, people and Prime Minister. Below this summit the builders of survival were Dowding, the architect of Fighter Command, Park, the foreman on the site, and Beaverbrook who miraculously supported all their efforts with new and repaired fighters. Each of these men suffered subsequently from the shafts of hind-sight criticising. It was complained that Park and implicitly Dowding, let the enemy through too often, had not killed enough Germans and would not listen to advice; that Beaverbrook recklessly interrupted long term programmes of the aircraft industry to produce his fighters. Yet with survival at stake, were Dowding and Park likely to overlook any practical proposition? Was Beaverbrook, who in fact gave every possible con-

The victor

sideration to the coming generation of heavy four-engine bombers, likely to get his priorities wrong?

Criticism of Park and thus indirectly of Dowding and the overall direction of Fighter Command came principally from one quarter.

As the battle warmed in July the natural frustration of No 11 Group pilots who felt infuriatingly reined-in was as nothing compared to that in No 12 Group where there was resentment. Whereas Park's pilots grumbled because they were only allowed 'to get at them' in very small numbers, Air Vice-Marshal Leigh-Mallory's Squadrons thought they were missing a war while England fell. In aggravation of this understandable exasperation at Squadron level, the Group commander was a naturally aggressive leader, spoiling for a fight. But Dowding had built a very carefully thought-out system of defence and in that system the key man, Park, was a defensive fighter, making his moves with an eye on the morrow.

Could the RAF have done better with Leigh-Mallory in Park's place? Leigh-Mallory thought so. He pressed for the big wing, five Squadron formations of sixty fighters like the formation he eventually sent sweeping over London on September 15 and which chased the enemy from Westminster to the sea. Yet a tactic that happened to serve successfully in the conditions of September 15 would have courted disaster in July and August.

True the big wings might have increased the kill once they had assembled and located the enemy. But while they were climbing, joining up and finding the enemy, irreparable damage would have been done to the airfields under attack. Assembly, incidentally, was fraught with difficulty at this stage of the war when Squadrons were unable to communicate with each other in the air. Further, to offer the Luftwaffe big wings composed of a high percentage of the RAF's operational strength would have assisted the enemy's scheme to eliminate fighter resistance over the invasion corner of England. Small though Park's intercepting forces were in the earlier weeks of the battle they managed repeatedly to break up enemy formations and often to distract escorting fighters, leaving

the bomber force open to attack When, later in the battle Park began to pair Squadrons and even to assemble larger formations it was not because of pressure from No 12 Group but because the Luftwaffe's tactics were changing. When the introduction of fighter-bombers called for readiness patrols at heights above twenty thousand feet, the time factor in assembly of a wing was not so pressing.

For all this, in November 1940, higher authority was attracted to the big wing theory and allowed itself to be carried away by an exciting portrayal of what might have been and what could be in the future.

When invasion was no longer likely, when daylight raiders had been driven out of Britain's skies by winter weather, Dowding, somewhat shabbily – though now aged sixty – received the 'bowler hat' which he himself had half expected since the start of it all in 1936.

On November 25 Dowding was succeeded by Air Marshal Sholto Douglas, later promoted Marshal of the Royal Air Force, an honour that Dowding was never accorded. Shortly after-

The vanquished

158

ward, Park was replaced by Leigh-Mallory who had been breathing down his neck for so long – injustices which were only partly atoned by Dowding's subsequent elevation to the peerage and Park's important commands in Malta and South East Asia. Yet, between them, Dowding and Park's contribution to national survival had equalled, if not surpassed, the record of Horatio Nelson at Trafalgar, Britain's greatest hero before their time.

And what of Beaverbrook, the third man of the trio? Churchill and Dowding have left posterity in no doubt of their opinion of the newspaper millionaire from Fleet Street who produced the fighters. Dowding rated Beaverbrook's appointment as 'magical' and as of equal importance to Churchill's veto on fighter reinforcements for France in May, 1940. Churchill needed his 'vital and vibrant energy.'

Beaverbrook, wealthy, powerful, aged 61, was driven by a fresh incentive. 'London has many lamp posts' he said 'Hitler has reserved one for me – and that is where I would have been hanging if I had not produced the fighters.'

In the end, it was Britain, Russia and the United States that did the hanging, though Hermann Goering, so near success in August and September 1940, escaped when he cheated the hangman with a poison capsule.

When all is said and done the significance of the providential defeat of the Luftwaffe by the Royal Air Force in the Battle of Britain of 1940 can be summed up in a sentence:

But for British victory the German army would have occupied London and within weeks, among many other oppressive measures, Germany would have activated SS Colonel Professor Dr Six's programme for the deportation of able-bodied men between the ages of seventeen and forty-five.

Without air cover it is unlikely that the Royal Navy would have managed to control the sea.

The message of the Battle of Britain is unequivocably that under the national inspiration of Winston Churchill 'The Few' saved the British people from being enslaved by Germany.

Bibliography

Reach for the Sky Paul Brickhill (Collins, London)
The Second World War Winston S Churchill (Cassell, London)
Speeches Winston S Churchill (Cassell, London)
Secret Session Speeches Winston S Churchill (Cassell, London)
Leading the Few Basil Collier (Jarrolds, London)
The Defence of the United Kingdom Basil Collier (HMSO, London)
Eagle Day Richard Collier (Hodder and Stoughton, London)
Nine Lives Group Captain A C Deere (Hodder and Stoughton, London)
Invasion 1940 Peter Fleming (Hart-Davis, London)
The First and the Last Adolf Galland (Methuen, London. Holt, New York)
The Last Enemy Richard Hillary (Macmillan, London) US title *Falling Through Space* (Reynat and Hitchcock, New York)
Wing Leader J E Johnson (Chatto and Windus, London)
British War Production M M Postan (HMSO, London)
The Struggle for Europe Chester Wilmot (Collins, London)
The Narrow Margin D Wood & D Dempster (Hutchinson, London)
Fighter Command Air Vice-Marshal P G Wyetham (Putnam, London)
Royal Air Force 1939-1945 Vol. I Denis Richards (HMSO, London)